W9-BAF-596

THE RULES OF GOLF

as approved by
THE UNITED STATES GOLF ASSOCIATION®
and
The R&A

Effective January 1, 2010

Cover photo:
*Arnold Palmer during the 1963 U.S. Open Championship
at The Country Club in Brookline, Mass. © Bob Gomel*

Mixed Sources
Product group from well-managed
forests, controlled sources and
recycled wood or fiber
www.fsc.org Cert no. SW-COC-002134
© 1996 Forest Stewardship Council
FSC

HOW TO USE THE RULES BOOK

UNDERSTAND THE WORDS

The Rules book is written in a very precise and deliberate fashion. You should be aware of and understand the following differences in word use:

may = optional

should = recommendation

must = instruction (and penalty if not carried out)

a ball = you may substitute another ball (e.g., Rules 26, 27 and 28)

the ball = you may not substitute another ball (e.g., Rules 24-2 and 25-1)

KNOW THE DEFINITIONS

There are over 50 defined terms and these form the foundation on which the Rules of Play are written. A good knowledge of the defined terms (which are italicized throughout the book) is very important to the correct application of the Rules.

WHICH RULE APPLIES?

The Contents pages may help you find the relevant Rule; alternatively, there is an Index at the back of the book.

WHAT IS THE RULING?

To answer any question on the Rules you must first establish the facts of the case.

To do so you should identify:

1. The form of play (e.g., match play or stroke play; single, foursome or four-ball?).
2. Who is involved (e.g., the player, his partner or caddie, an outside agency?).
3. Where the incident occurred (e.g., on the teeing ground, in a bunker or water hazard, on the putting green or elsewhere on the course?).
4. The player's intentions (e.g., what was he doing and what does he want to do?).
5. Any subsequent events (e.g., the player has returned his score card or the competition has closed).

REFER TO THE BOOK

It is recommended that you carry a Rules book in your golf bag and use it whenever a question arises. If in doubt, play the course as you find it and play the ball as it lies. Once back in the Clubhouse, reference to "Decisions on the Rules of Golf" should help resolve any outstanding queries.

FOREWORD FROM THE CHAIRMEN

This book contains the Rules of Golf as approved jointly by the United States Golf Association and The R&A. The Rules are revised on a four-year cycle, and the next revision will take effec January 1, 2012.

We hope you will carry a Rules book in your golf bag and refer to it as necessary.

The USGA wishes to thank Rolex for its continued generous funding of this publication.

James T. Bunch   Alan W. J. Holmes
Chairman   Chairman
Rules of Golf Committee   Rules of Golf Committee
United States Golf Association   The R&A

The USGA publication entitled "A Modification of the Rules of Golf for Golfers with Disabilities" that contains permissible modifications to The Rules of Golf to accommodate disabled golfers is available through the USGA.

PRINCIPAL CHANGE

Appendix II

Impact Area Markings (5c) – Amended to include new requirements for groove and punch mark conformance.

CONTENTS

Relief Situations and Procedure

Other Forms of Play

Administration

Appendix I: Local Rules; Conditions of the Competition

In the Rules of Golf, the gender used in relation to any person is understood to include both genders.

SECTION I ETIQUETTE; BEHAVIOR ON THE COURSE

Introduction

This Section provides guidelines on the manner in which the game of golf should be played. If they are followed, all players will gain maximum enjoyment from the game. The overriding principle is that consideration should be shown to others on the course at all times.

The Spirit of the Game

Golf is played, for the most part, without the supervision of a referee or umpire. The game relies on the integrity of the individual to show consideration for other players and to abide by the Rules. All players should conduct themselves in a disciplined manner, demonstrating courtesy and sportsmanship at all times, irrespective of how competitive they may be. This is the spirit of the game of golf.

Safety

Players should ensure that no one is standing close by or in a position to be hit by the club, the ball or any stones, pebbles, twigs or the like when they make a stroke or practice swing.

Players should not play until the players in front are out of range.

Players should always alert greenstaff nearby or ahead when they are about to make a stroke that might endanger them.

If a player plays a ball in a direction where there is a danger of hitting someone, he should immediately shout a warning. The traditional word of warning in such situations is "fore."

Consideration for Other Players

No Disturbance or Distraction
Players should always show consideration for other players on the course and should not disturb their play by moving, talking or making unnecessary noise.

Players should ensure that any electronic device taken onto the course does not distract other players.

On the teeing ground, a player should not tee his ball until it is his turn to play.

Players should not stand close to or directly behind the ball, or directly behind the hole, when a player is about to play.

On the Putting Green
On the putting green, players should not stand on another player's line of putt or, when he is making a stroke, cast a shadow over his line of putt.

Players should remain on or close to the putting green until all other players in the group have holed out.

Scoring
In stroke play, a player who is acting as a marker should, if necessary, on the way to the next tee, check the score with the player concerned and record it.

Pace of Play

Play at Good Pace and Keep Up
Players should play at a good pace. The Committee may establish pace of play guidelines that all players should follow.

It is a group's responsibility to keep up with the group in front. If it loses a clear hole and it is delaying the group behind, it should invite the group behind to play through, irrespective of the number of players in that group. Where a group has not lost a clear hole, but it is apparent that the group behind can play faster, it should invite the faster moving group to play through.

Be Ready to Play

Players should be ready to play as soon as it is their turn to play. When playing on or near the putting green, they should leave their bags or carts in such a position as will enable quick movement off the green and towards the next tee. When the play of a hole has been completed, players should immediately leave the putting green.

Lost Ball

If a player believes his ball may be lost outside a water hazard or is out of bounds, to save time, he should play a provisional ball.

Players searching for a ball should signal the players in the group behind them to play through as soon as it becomes apparent that the ball will not easily be found. They should not search for five minutes before doing so. Having allowed the group behind to play through, they should not continue play until that group has passed and is out of range.

Priority on the Course

Unless otherwise determined by the Committee, priority on the course is determined by a group's pace of play. Any group playing a whole round is entitled to pass a group playing a shorter round. The term "group" includes a single player.

Care of the Course

Bunkers

Before leaving a bunker, players should carefully fill up and smooth over all holes and footprints made by them and any nearby made by others. If a rake is within reasonable proximity of the bunker, the rake should be used for this purpose.

Repair of Divots, Ball-Marks and Damage by Shoes

Players should carefully repair any divot holes made by them and any damage to the putting green made by the impact of a ball (whether or not made by the player himself). On completion of the hole by all players in the group, damage to the putting green caused by golf shoes should be repaired.

Preventing Unnecessary Damage

Players should avoid causing damage to the course by removing divots when taking practice swings or by hitting the head of a club into the ground, whether in anger or for any other reason.

Players should ensure that no damage is done to the putting green when putting down bags or the flagstick.

In order to avoid damaging the hole, players and caddies should not stand too close to the hole and should take care during the handling of the flagstick and the removal of a ball from the hole. The head of a club should not be used to remove a ball from the hole.

Players should not lean on their clubs when on the putting green, particularly when removing the ball from the hole.

The flagstick should be properly replaced in the hole before the players leave the putting green.

Local notices regulating the movement of golf carts should be strictly observed.

Conclusion; Penalties for Breach

If players follow the guidelines in this Section, it will make the game more enjoyable for everyone.

If a player consistently disregards these guidelines during a round or over a period of time to the detriment of others, it is recommended that the Committee consider taking appropriate disciplinary action against the offending player. Such action may, for example, include prohibiting play for a limited time on the course or in a certain number of competitions. This is considered to be justifiable in terms of protecting the interests of the majority of golfers who wish to play in accordance with these guidelines.

In the case of a serious breach of etiquette, the Committee may disqualify a player under Rule 33-7.

SECTION II DEFINITIONS

The Definitions are listed alphabetically and, in the *Rules* themselves, defined terms are in *italics*.

Abnormal Ground Conditions
An "*abnormal ground condition*" is any *casual water*, *ground under repair* or hole, cast or runway on the *course* made by a *burrowing animal*, a reptile or a bird.

Addressing the Ball
A player has "*addressed the ball*" when he has taken his *stance* and has also grounded his club, except that in a *hazard* a player has *addressed the ball* when he has taken his *stance*.

Advice
"*Advice*" is any counsel or suggestion that could influence a player in determining his play, the choice of a club or the method of making a *stroke*.

Information on the *Rules*, distance or matters of public information, such as the position of *hazards* or the *flagstick* on the *putting green*, is not *advice*.

Ball Deemed to Move
See "*Move* or *Moved*."

Ball Holed
See "*Holed*."

Ball Lost
See "*Lost Ball*."

Ball in Play
A ball is "*in play*" as soon as the player has made a *stroke* on the *teeing ground*. It remains *in play* until it is *holed*, except when it is *lost*, *out of bounds* or lifted, or another ball has been *substituted*, whether or not the substitution is permitted; a ball so *substituted* becomes the *ball in play*.

If a ball is played from outside the *teeing ground* when the player is starting play of a hole, or when attempting to correct this mistake, the ball is not *in play* and Rule 11-4 or 11-5 applies. Otherwise, *ball in play* includes a ball played from outside the *teeing ground* when the player elects or is required to play his next *stroke* from the *teeing ground*.

Exception in match play: *Ball in play* includes a ball played by the player from outside the *teeing ground* when starting play of a hole if the opponent does not require the *stroke* to be canceled in accordance with Rule 11-4a.

Best-Ball
See "*Forms of Match Play*."

Bunker
A "*bunker*" is a *hazard* consisting of a prepared area of ground, often a hollow, from which turf or soil has been removed and replaced with sand or the like.

Grass-covered ground bordering or within a *bunker,* including a stacked turf face (whether grass-covered or earthen), is not part of the *bunker.* A wall or lip of the *bunker* not covered with grass is part of the *bunker.* The margin of a *bunker* extends vertically downwards, but not upwards.

A ball is in a *bunker* when it lies in or any part of it touches the *bunker.*

Burrowing Animal
A "*burrowing animal*" is an animal (other than a worm, insect or the like) that makes a hole for habitation or shelter, such as a rabbit, mole, groundhog, gopher or salamander.

Note: A hole made by a non-burrowing animal, such as a dog, is not an *abnormal ground condition* unless marked or declared as *ground under repair.*

Caddie
A "*caddie*" is one who assists the player in accordance with the *Rules*, which may include carrying or handling the player's clubs during play.

When one *caddie* is employed by more than one player, he is always deemed to be the *caddie* of the player sharing the *caddie* whose ball (or whose *partner's* ball) is involved, and *equipment* carried by him is deemed to be that player's *equipment*, except when the *caddie* acts upon specific directions of another player (or the *partner* of another player) sharing the *caddie*, in which case he is considered to be that other player's *caddie*.

Casual Water

"*Casual water*" is any temporary accumulation of water on the *course* that is not in a *water hazard* and is visible before or after the player takes his *stance*. Snow and natural ice, other than frost, are either *casual water* or *loose impediments*, at the option of the player. Manufactured ice is an *obstruction*. Dew and frost are not *casual water*.

A ball is in *casual water* when it lies in or any part of it touches the *casual water*.

Committee

The "*Committee*" is the committee in charge of the competition or, if the matter does not arise in a competition, the committee in charge of the *course*.

Competitor

A "*competitor*" is a player in a stroke-play competition. A "*fellow-competitor*" is any person with whom the *competitor* plays. Neither is *partner* of the other.

In stroke-play *foursome* and *four-ball* competitions, where the context so admits, the word "*competitor*" or "*fellow-competitor*" includes his *partner*.

Course

The "*course*" is the whole area within any boundaries established by the *Committee* (see Rule 33-2).

Equipment

"*Equipment*" is anything used, worn or carried by the player or anything carried for the player by his *partner* or either of their *caddies*, except any ball he has played at the hole being played and any small object, such as a coin or a *tee,* when used to mark the position of a ball or the extent of an area in which a ball is to be dropped. *Equipment* includes a golf cart, whether or not motorized.

Note 1: A ball played at the hole being played is *equipment* when it has been lifted and not put back into play.

Note 2: When a golf cart is shared by two or more players, the cart and everything in it are deemed to be the *equipment* of one of the players sharing the cart.

If the cart is being moved by one of the players (or the *partner* of one of the players) sharing it, the cart and everything in it are deemed to be that player's *equipment*. Otherwise, the cart and everything in it are deemed to be the *equipment* of the player sharing the cart whose ball (or whose *partner's* ball) is involved.

Fellow-Competitor
See "*Competitor*."

Flagstick
The "*flagstick*" is a movable straight indicator, with or without bunting or other material attached, centered in the *hole* to show its position. It must be circular in cross-section. Padding or shock absorbent material that might unduly influence the movement of the ball is prohibited.

Forecaddie
A "*forecaddie*" is one who is employed by the *Committee* to indicate to players the position of balls during play. He is an *outside agency*.

Forms of Match Play
Single: A match in which one player plays against another player.

Threesome: A match in which one player plays against two other players, and each *side* plays one ball.

Foursome: A match in which two players play against two other players, and each *side* plays one ball.

Three-Ball: Three players play a match against one another, each playing his own ball. Each player is playing two distinct matches.

Best-Ball: A match in which one player plays against the better ball of two other players or the best ball of three other players.

Four-Ball: A match in which two players play their better ball against the better ball of two other players.

Forms of Stroke Play

Individual: A competition in which each *competitor* plays as an individual.

Foursome: A competition in which two *competitors* play as *partners* and play one ball.

Four-Ball: A competition in which two *competitors* play as *partners*, each playing his own ball. The lower score of the *partners* is the score for the hole. If one *partner* fails to complete the play of the hole, there is no penalty.

Note: For bogey, par and Stableford competitions, see Rule 32-1.

Four-Ball

See "*Forms of Match Play*" and "*Forms of Stroke Play.*"

Foursome

See "*Forms of Match Play*" and "*Forms of Stroke Play.*"

Ground Under Repair

"*Ground under repair*" is any part of the *course* so marked by order of the *Committee* or so declared by its authorized representative. All ground and any grass, bush, tree or other growing thing within the *ground under repair* are part of the *ground under repair*. *Ground under repair* includes material piled for removal and a hole made by a greenkeeper, even if not so marked. Grass cuttings and other material left on the *course* that have been abandoned and are not intended to be removed are not *ground under repair* unless so marked.

When the margin of *ground under repair* is defined by stakes, the stakes are inside the *ground under repair*, and the margin of the *ground under repair* is defined by the nearest outside points of the stakes at ground level. When both stakes and lines are used to indicate *ground under repair*, the stakes identify the *ground under repair* and the lines define the margin of the *ground under repair*. When the margin of *ground under repair* is defined by a line on the ground, the line itself is in the *ground under repair*. The margin of *ground under repair* extends vertically downwards but not upwards.

A ball is in *ground under repair* when it lies in or any part of it touches the *ground under repair*.

Stakes used to define the margin of or identify *ground under repair* are *obstructions*.

Note: The *Committee* may make a Local Rule prohibiting play from *ground under repair* or an environmentally-sensitive area defined as *ground under repair*.

Hazards
A "*hazard*" is any *bunker* or *water hazard*.

Hole
The "*hole*" must be 4¼ inches (108 mm) in diameter and at least 4 inches (101.6 mm) deep. If a lining is used, it must be sunk at least 1 inch (25.4 mm) below the *putting green* surface, unless the nature of the soil makes it impracticable to do so; its outer diameter must not exceed 4¼ inches (108 mm).

Holed
A ball is "*holed*" when it is at rest within the circumference of the *hole* and all of it is below the level of the lip of the *hole*.

Honor
The player who is to play first from the *teeing ground* is said to have the "*honor*."

Lateral Water Hazard
A "*lateral water hazard*" is a *water hazard* or that part of a *water hazard* so situated that it is not possible, or is deemed by the *Committee* to be impracticable, to drop a ball behind the *water hazard* in accordance with Rule 26-1b. All ground and water within the margin of a *lateral water hazard* are part of the *lateral water hazard*.

When the margin of a *lateral water hazard* is defined by stakes, the stakes are inside the *lateral water hazard*, and the margin of the *hazard* is defined by the nearest outside points of the stakes at ground level. When both stakes and lines are used to indicate a *lateral water hazard*, the stakes identify the *hazard* and the lines define the *hazard* margin. When the margin of a *lateral water hazard* is defined by a line on the ground, the line itself is in the *lateral water hazard*. The margin of a *lateral water hazard* extends vertically upwards and downwards.

A ball is in a *lateral water hazard* when it lies in or any part of it touches the *lateral water hazard*.

Stakes used to define the margin of or identify a *lateral water hazard* are *obstructions*.

Note 1: That part of a *water hazard* to be played as a *lateral water hazard* must be distinctively marked. Stakes or lines used to define the margin of or identify a *lateral water hazard* must be red.

Note 2: The *Committee* may make a Local Rule prohibiting play from an environmentally-sensitive area defined as a *lateral water hazard*.

Note 3: The *Committee* may define a *lateral water hazard* as a *water hazard*.

Line of Play

The "*line of play*" is the direction that the player wishes his ball to take after a *stroke*, plus a reasonable distance on either side of the intended direction. The *line of play* extends vertically upwards from the ground, but does not extend beyond the *hole*.

Line of Putt

The "*line of putt*" is the line that the player wishes his ball to take after a *stroke* on the *putting green*. Except with respect to Rule 16-1e, the *line of putt* includes a reasonable distance on either side of the intended line. The *line of putt* does not extend beyond the *hole*.

Loose Impediments

"*Loose impediments*" are natural objects including:

- stones, leaves, twigs, branches and the like,
- dung, and
- worms, insects and the like, and the casts and heaps made by them,

provided they are not:

- fixed or growing,
- solidly embedded, or
- adhering to the ball.

Sand and loose soil are *loose impediments* on the *putting green*, but not elsewhere.

Snow and natural ice, other than frost, are either *casual water* or *loose impediments*, at the option of the player.

Dew and frost are not *loose impediments*.

Lost Ball

A ball is deemed "*lost*" if:

a. It is not found or identified as his by the player within five minutes after the player's *side* or his or their *caddies* have begun to search for it; or

b. The player has made a *stroke* at a *provisional ball* from the place where the original ball is likely to be or from a point nearer the *hole* than that place (see Rule 27-2b); or

c. The player has put another ball into play under penalty of stroke and distance (see Rule 27-1a); or

d. The player has put another ball into play because it is known or virtually certain that the ball, which has not been found, has been moved by an *outside agency* (see Rule 18-1), is in an *obstruction* (see Rule 24-3), is in an *abnormal ground condition* (see Rule 25-1c) or is in a *water hazard* (see Rule 26-1); or

e. The player has made a *stroke* at a *substituted* ball.

Time spent in playing a *wrong ball* is not counted in the five-minute period allowed for search.

Marker

A "*marker*" is one who is appointed by the *Committee* to record a *competitor's* score in stroke play. He may be a *fellow-competitor*. He is not a *referee*.

Move or Moved

A ball is deemed to have "*moved*" if it leaves its position and comes to rest in any other place.

Nearest Point of Relief

The "*nearest point of relief*" is the reference point for taking relief without penalty from interference by an immovable *obstruction* (Rule 24-2), an *abnormal ground condition* (Rule 25-1) or a *wrong putting green* (Rule 25-3).

It is the point on the *course* nearest to where the ball lies:

(i) that is not nearer the *hole,* and

(ii) where, if the ball were so positioned, no interference by the condition from which relief is sought would exist for the *stroke* the player would have made from the original position if the condition were not there.

Note: In order to determine the *nearest point of relief* accurately, the player should use the club with which he would have made his next *stroke* if the condition were not there to simulate the *address* position, direction of play and swing for such a *stroke*.

Observer

An "*observer*" is one who is appointed by the *Committee* to assist a *referee* to decide questions of fact and to report to him any breach of a *Rule*. An *observer* should not attend the *flagstick*, stand at or mark the position of the *hole*, or lift the ball or mark its position.

Obstructions

An "*obstruction*" is anything artificial, including the artificial surfaces and sides of roads and paths and manufactured ice, except:

a. Objects defining *out of bounds*, such as walls, fences, stakes and railings;

b. Any part of an immovable artificial object that is *out of bounds*; and

c. Any construction declared by the *Committee* to be an integral part of the *course*.

An *obstruction* is a movable *obstruction* if it may be moved without unreasonable effort, without unduly delaying play and without causing damage. Otherwise, it is an immovable *obstruction*.

Note: The *Committee* may make a Local Rule declaring a movable *obstruction* to be an immovable *obstruction*.

Out of Bounds

"*Out of bounds*" is beyond the boundaries of the *course* or any part of the *course* so marked by the *Committee*.

When *out of bounds* is defined by reference to stakes or a fence or as being beyond stakes or a fence, the *out of bounds* line is determined by the nearest inside points at ground level of the stakes or fence posts (excluding angled supports). When both stakes and lines are used to indicate *out of bounds*, the stakes identify *out of bounds* and the lines define *out of bounds*. When *out of bounds* is defined by a line on the ground, the line itself is *out of bounds*. The *out of bounds* line extends vertically upwards and downwards.

A ball is *out of bounds* when all of it lies *out of bounds*. A player may stand *out of bounds* to play a ball lying within bounds.

Objects defining *out of bounds* such as walls, fences, stakes and railings, are not *obstructions* and are deemed to be fixed. Stakes identifying *out of bounds* are not *obstructions* and are deemed to be fixed.

Note 1: Stakes or lines used to define *out of bounds* should be white.

Note 2: A *Committee* may make a Local Rule declaring stakes identifying but not defining *out of bounds* to be movable *obstructions*.

Outside Agency

In match play, an "*outside agency*" is any agency other than either the player's or opponent's *side*, any *caddie* of either *side*, any ball played by either *side* at the hole being played or any *equipment* of either *side*.

In stroke play, an *outside agency* is any agency other than the *competitor's side*, any *caddie* of the *side*, any ball played by the *side* at the hole being played or any *equipment* of the *side*.

An *outside agency* includes a *referee*, a *marker*, an *observer* and a *forecaddie*. Neither wind nor water is an *outside agency*.

Partner

A "*partner*" is a player associated with another player on the same *side*.

In *threesome*, *foursome*, *best-ball* or *four-ball* play, where the context so admits, the word "player" includes his *partner* or *partners*.

Penalty Stroke

A "*penalty stroke*" is one added to the score of a player or *side* under certain *Rules*. In a *threesome* or *foursome*, *penalty strokes* do not affect the order of play.

Provisional Ball

A "*provisional ball*" is a ball played under Rule 27-2 for a ball that may be *lost* outside a *water hazard* or may be *out of bounds*.

Putting Green

The "*putting green*" is all ground of the hole being played that is specially prepared for putting or otherwise defined as such by the *Committee*. A ball is on the *putting green* when any part of it touches the *putting green*.

Referee

A "*referee*" is one who is appointed by the *Committee* to accompany players to decide questions of fact and apply the *Rules*. He must act on any breach of a *Rule* that he observes or is reported to him.

A *referee* should not attend the *flagstick*, stand at or mark the position of the *hole*, or lift the ball or mark its position.

Rub of the Green

A "*rub of the green*" occurs when a ball in motion is accidentally deflected or stopped by any *outside agency* (see Rule 19-1).

Rule or Rules

The term "*Rule*" includes:

a. The Rules of Golf and their interpretations as contained in "Decisions on the Rules of Golf";

b. Any Conditions of Competition established by the *Committee* under Rule 33-1 and Appendix I;

c. Any Local Rules established by the *Committee* under Rule 33-8a and Appendix I; and

d. The specifications on clubs and the ball in Appendices II and III and their interpretations as contained in "A Guide to the Rules on Clubs and Balls."

Side

A "*side*" is a player, or two or more players who are *partners*.

Single

See "*Forms of Match Play*" and "*Forms of Stroke Play*."

Stance

Taking the "*stance*" consists in a player placing his feet in position for and preparatory to making a *stroke*.

Stipulated Round

The "*stipulated round*" consists of playing the holes of the *course* in their correct sequence, unless otherwise authorized by the *Committee*. The number of holes in a *stipulated round* is 18 unless a smaller number is authorized by the *Committee*. As to extension of *stipulated round* in match play, see Rule 2-3.

Stroke

A "*stroke*" is the forward movement of the club made with the intention of striking at and moving the ball, but if a player checks his downswing voluntarily before the clubhead reaches the ball he has not made a *stroke*.

Substituted Ball

A "*substituted ball*" is a ball put into play for the original ball that was either *in play, lost, out of bounds* or lifted.

Tee

A "*tee*" is a device designed to raise the ball off the ground. It must not be longer than 4 inches (101.6 mm), and it must not be designed or manufactured in such a way that it could indicate the *line of play* or influence the movement of the ball.

Teeing Ground

The "*teeing ground*" is the starting place for the hole to be played. It is a rectangular area two club-lengths in depth, the front and the sides of which are defined by the outside limits of two tee-markers. A ball is outside the *teeing ground* when all of it lies outside the *teeing ground*.

Three-Ball
See "*Forms of Match Play.*"

Threesome
See "*Forms of Match Play.*"

Through the Green
"*Through the green*" is the whole area of the *course* except:

   a. The *teeing ground* and *putting green* of the hole being played; and

   b. All *hazards* on the *course*.

Water Hazard
A "*water hazard*" is any sea, lake, pond, river, ditch, surface drainage ditch or other open water course (whether or not containing water) and anything of a similar nature on the *course*. All ground and water within the margin of a *water hazard* are part of the *water hazard*.

When the margin of a *water hazard* is defined by stakes, the stakes are inside the *water hazard*, and the margin of the *hazard* is defined by the nearest outside points of the stakes at ground level. When both stakes and lines are used to indicate a *water hazard*, the stakes identify the *hazard* and the lines define the *hazard* margin. When the margin of a *water hazard* is defined by a line on the ground, the line itself is in the *water hazard*. The margin of a *water hazard* extends vertically upwards and downwards.

A ball is in a *water hazard* when it lies in or any part of it touches the *water hazard*.

Stakes used to define the margin of or identify a *water hazard* are *obstructions*.

Note 1: Stakes or lines used to define the margin of or identify a *water hazard* must be yellow.

Note 2: The *Committee* may make a Local Rule prohibiting play from an environmentally-sensitive area defined as a *water hazard*.

Wrong Ball

A *"wrong ball"* is any ball other than the player's:

- *ball in play*;
- *provisional ball*; or
- second ball played under Rule 3-3 or Rule 20-7c in stroke play;

and includes:

- another player's ball;
- an abandoned ball; and
- the player's original ball when it is no longer *in play*.

Note: *Ball in play* includes a ball *substituted* for the *ball in play*, whether or not the substitution is permitted.

Wrong Putting Green

A *"wrong putting green"* is any *putting green* other than that of the hole being played. Unless otherwise prescribed by the *Committee*, this term includes a practice *putting green* or pitching green on the *course*.

SECTION III THE RULES OF PLAY

THE GAME

Rule 1. The Game

Definitions

All defined terms are in *italics* and are listed alphabetically in the Definitions section — see pages 5-18.

1-1. General

The Game of Golf consists of playing a ball with a club from the *teeing ground* into the *hole* by a *stroke* or successive *strokes* in accordance with the *Rules*.

1-2. Exerting Influence on Ball

A player or *caddie* must not take any action to influence the position or the movement of a ball except in accordance with the *Rules*.

(Removal of loose impediment — see Rule 23-1.)

(Removal of movable obstruction — see Rule 24-1.)

*PENALTY FOR BREACH OF RULE 1-2:

<u>Match play</u> — Loss of hole; <u>Stroke play</u> — Two strokes.

*In the case of a serious breach of Rule 1-2, the *Committee* may impose a penalty of disqualification.

Note: A player is deemed to have committed a serious breach of Rule 1-2 if the *Committee* considers that his act of influencing the position or movement of the ball has allowed him or another player to gain a significant advantage or has placed another player, other than his *partner*, at a significant disadvantage.

1-3. Agreement to Waive Rules

Players must not agree to exclude the operation of any *Rule* or to waive any penalty incurred.

PENALTY FOR BREACH OF RULE 1-3:

<u>Match play</u> — Disqualification of both *sides*;

<u>Stroke play</u> — Disqualification of *competitors* concerned.

(Agreeing to play out of turn in stroke play — see Rule 10-2c.)

1-4. Points Not Covered by Rules

If any point in dispute is not covered by the *Rules*, the decision should be made in accordance with equity.

Rule 2. Match Play

Definitions

All defined terms are in *italics* and are listed alphabetically in the Definitions section — see pages 5-18.

2-1. General

A match consists of one *side* playing against another over a *stipulated round* unless otherwise decreed by the *Committee*.

In match play the game is played by holes.

Except as otherwise provided in the *Rules*, a hole is won by the *side* that *holes* its ball in the fewer *strokes*. In a handicap match, the lower net score wins the hole.

The state of the match is expressed by the terms: so many "holes up" or "all square," and so many "to play."

A *side* is "dormie" when it is as many holes up as there are holes remaining to be played.

2-2. Halved Hole

A hole is halved if each *side holes* out in the same number of *strokes*.

When a player has *holed* out and his opponent has been left with a *stroke* for the half, if the player subsequently incurs a penalty, the hole is halved.

2-3. Winner of Match

A match is won when one *side* leads by a number of holes greater than the number remaining to be played.

If there is a tie, the *Committee* may extend the *stipulated round* by as many holes as are required for a match to be won.

2-4. Concession of Match, Hole or Next Stroke

A player may concede a match at any time prior to the st̲a̲r̲t̲ o̲r̲ conclusion of that match.

A player may concede a hole at any time prior to the start or conclusion of that hole.

A player may concede his opponent's next *stroke* at any time, provided the opponent's ball is at rest. The opponent is considered to have *holed* out with his next *stroke*, and the ball may be removed by either *side*.

A concession may not be declined or withdrawn.

(Ball overhanging hole — see Rule 16-2.)

2-5. Doubt as to Procedure; Disputes and Claims

In match play, if a doubt or dispute arises between the players, a player may make a claim. If no duly authorized representative of the *Committee* is available within a reasonable time, the players must continue the match without delay. The *Committee* may consider a claim only if the player making the claim notifies his opponent (i) that he is making a claim, (ii) of the facts of the situation and (iii) that he wants a ruling. The claim must be made before any player in the match plays from the next *teeing ground* or, in the case of the last hole of the match, before all players in the match leave the *putting green*.

A later claim may not be considered by the *Committee*, unless it is based on facts previously unknown to the player making the claim and he had been given wrong information (Rules 6-2a and 9) by an opponent.

Once the result of the match has been officially announced, a later claim may not be considered by the *Committee*, unless it is satisfied that the opponent knew he was giving wrong information.

2-6. General Penalty

The penalty for a breach of a *Rule* in match play is loss of hole except when otherwise provided.

Rule 3. Stroke Play

are in italics and are listed alphabetically in ...ection — see pages 5-18.

3-1. Ge... Winner

A stroke-play competition consists of *competitors* completing each hole of a *stipulated round* or *rounds* and, for each round, returning a score card on which there is a gross score for each hole. Each *competitor* is playing against every other *competitor* in the competition.

The *competitor* who plays the *stipulated round* or *rounds* in the fewest *strokes* is the winner.

In a handicap competition, the *competitor* with the lowest net score for the *stipulated round* or *rounds* is the winner.

3-2. Failure to Hole Out

If a *competitor* fails to *hole out* at any hole and does not correct his mistake before he makes a *stroke* on the next *teeing ground* or, in the case of the last hole of the round, before he leaves the *putting green*, he is disqualified.

3-3. Doubt as to Procedure

a. Procedure

In stroke play, if a *competitor* is doubtful of his rights or the correct procedure during the play of a hole, he may, without penalty, complete the hole with two balls.

After the doubtful situation has arisen and before taking further action, the *competitor* must announce to his *marker* or a *fellow-competitor* that he intends to play two balls and which ball he wishes to count if the *Rules* permit.

The *competitor* must report the facts of the situation to the *Committee* before returning his score card. If he fails to do so, he is disqualified.

Note: If the *competitor* takes further action before dealing with the doubtful situation, Rule 3-3 is not applicable. The score with the original ball counts or, if the original ball is not one of the balls being played, the score with the first ball put into play counts, even if the *Rules* do not allow the procedure adopted for that ball. However, the *competitor* incurs no penalty for having played a second ball, and any *penalty strokes* incurred solely by playing that ball do not count in his score.

  b. Determination of Score for Hole
  (i) If the ball that the *competitor* selected in advance to count has been played in accordance with the *Rules,* the score with that ball is the *competitor's* score for the hole. Otherwise, the score with the other ball counts if the *Rules* allow the procedure adopted for that ball.

  (ii) If the *competitor* fails to announce in advance his decision to complete the hole with two balls, or which ball he wishes to count, the score with the original ball counts, provided it has been played in accordance with the *Rules.* If the original ball is not one of the balls being played, the first ball put into play counts, provided it has been played in accordance with the *Rules.* Otherwise, the score with the other ball counts if the *Rules* allow the procedure adopted for that ball.

Note 1: If a *competitor* plays a second ball under Rule 3-3, the *strokes* made after this Rule has been invoked with the ball ruled not to count and *penalty strokes* incurred solely by playing that ball are disregarded.

Note 2: A second ball played under Rule 3-3 is not a *provisional ball* under Rule 27-2.

3-4. Refusal to Comply with a Rule

If a *competitor* refuses to comply with a *Rule* affecting the rights of another *competitor*, he is disqualified.

3-5. General Penalty

The penalty for a breach of a *Rule* in stroke play is two strokes except when otherwise provided.

CLUBS AND THE BALL

The United States Golf Association (USGA) reserves the right, at any time, to change the Rules relating to clubs and balls (see Appendices II and III) and make or change the interpretations relating to these Rules.

Rule 4. Clubs

A player in doubt as to the conformity of a club should consult the USGA.

A manufacturer should submit to the USGA a sample of a club to be manufactured for a ruling as to whether the club conforms with the *Rules*. The sample becomes the property of the USGA for reference purposes. If a manufacturer fails to submit a sample or, having submitted a sample, fails to await a ruling before manufacturing and/or marketing the club, the manufacturer assumes the risk of a ruling that the club does not conform with the *Rules*.

Definitions

All defined terms are in *italics* and are listed alphabetically in the Definitions section — see pages 5-18.

4-1. Form and Make of Clubs

a. General

The player's clubs must conform with this Rule and the provisions, specifications and interpretations set forth in Appendix II.

Note: The *Committee* may require, in the conditions of a competition (Rule 33-1), that any driver the player carries must have a clubhead, identified by model and loft, that is named on the current List of Conforming Driver Heads issued by the USGA.

b. Wear and Alteration

A club that conforms with the *Rules* when new is deemed to conform after wear through normal use. Any part of a club that has been purposely altered is regarded as new and must, in its altered state, conform with the *Rules*.

4-2. Playing Characteristics Changed and Foreign Material

a. Playing Characteristics Changed

During a *stipulated round*, the playing characteristics of a club must not be purposely changed by adjustment or by any other means.

b. Foreign Material

Foreign material must not be applied to the club face for the purpose of influencing the movement of the ball.

*PENALTY FOR CARRYING, BUT NOT MAKING STROKE WITH, CLUB OR CLUBS IN BREACH OF RULE 4-1 or 4-2:

Match play — At the conclusion of the hole at which the breach is discovered, the state of the match is adjusted by deducting one hole for each hole at which a breach occurred; maximum deduction per round — Two holes.

Stroke play — Two strokes for each hole at which any breach occurred; maximum penalty per round — Four strokes.

Match or stroke play — In the event of a breach between the play of two holes, the penalty applies to the next hole.

Bogey and par competitions — See Note 1 to Rule 32-1a.

Stableford competitions — See Note 1 to Rule 32-1b.

*Any club or clubs carried in breach of Rule 4-1 or 4-2 must be declared out of play by the player to his opponent in match play or his *marker* or a *fellow-competitor* in stroke play immediately upon discovery that a breach has occurred. If the player fails to do so, he is disqualified.

PENALTY FOR MAKING STROKE WITH CLUB IN BREACH OF RULE 4-1 or 4-2: Disqualification.

4-3. Damaged Clubs: Repair and Replacement

a. Damage in Normal Course of Play

If, during a *stipulated round*, a player's club is damaged in the normal course of play, he may:

(i) use the club in its damaged state for the remainder of the *stipulated round*; or

(ii) without unduly delaying play, repair it or have it repaired; or

(iii) as an additional option available only if the club is unfit for play, replace the damaged club with any club. The replacement of a club must not unduly delay play and must not be made by borrowing any club selected for play by any other person playing on the *course*.

PENALTY FOR BREACH OF RULE 4-3a:
See Penalty Statements for Rule 4-4a or b and Rule 4-4c.

Note: A club is unfit for play if it is substantially damaged, e.g., the shaft is dented, significantly bent or broken into pieces; the clubhead becomes loose, detached or significantly deformed; or the grip becomes loose. A club is not unfit for play solely because the club's lie or loft has been altered, or the clubhead is scratched.

b. Damage Other Than in Normal Course of Play

If, during a *stipulated round*, a player's club is damaged other than in the normal course of play rendering it non-conforming or changing its playing characteristics, the club must not subsequently be used or replaced during the round.

c. Damage Prior to Round

A player may use a club damaged prior to a round, provided the club, in its damaged state, conforms with the *Rules*.

Damage to a club that occurred prior to a round may be repaired during the round, provided the playing characteristics are not changed and play is not unduly delayed.

PENALTY FOR BREACH OF RULE 4-3b or c: Disqualification.

(Undue delay — see Rule 6-7.)

4-4. Maximum of 14 Clubs

a. Selection and Addition of Clubs

The player must not start a *stipulated round* with more than 14 clubs. He is limited to the clubs thus selected for that round, except that if he started with fewer than 14 clubs, he may add any number, provided his total number does not exceed 14.

The addition of a club or clubs must not unduly delay play

(Rule 6-7) and the player must not add or borrow any club selected for play by any other person playing on the *course*.

b. Partners May Share Clubs

Partners may share clubs, provided that the total number of clubs carried by the *partners* so sharing does not exceed 14.

PENALTY FOR BREACH OF RULE 4-4a or b, REGARDLESS OF NUMBER OF EXCESS CLUBS CARRIED:

Match play — At the conclusion of the hole at which the breach is discovered, the state of the match is adjusted by deducting one hole for each hole at which a breach occurred; maximum deduction per round: Two holes.

Stroke play — Two strokes for each hole at which any breach occurred; maximum penalty per round: Four strokes.

Bogey and par competitions — See Note 1 to Rule 32-1a.

Stableford competitions — See Note 1 to Rule 32-1b.

c. Excess Club Declared Out of Play

Any club or clubs carried or used in breach of Rule 4-3a(iii) or Rule 4-4 must be declared out of play by the player to his opponent in match play or his *marker* or a *fellow-competitor* in stroke play immediately upon discovery that a breach has occurred. The player must not use the club or clubs for the remainder of the *stipulated round*.

PENALTY FOR BREACH OF RULE 4-4c: Disqualification.

Rule 5. The Ball

Definitions

All defined terms are in *italics* and are listed alphabetically in the Definitions section — see pages 5-18.

5-1. General

The ball the player plays must conform to the requirements specified in Appendix III.

Note: The *Committee* may require, in the conditions of a competition (Rule 33-1), that the ball the player plays must be named on the current List of Conforming Golf Balls issued by the United States Golf Association.

5-2. Foreign Material

Foreign material must not be applied to a ball for the purpose of changing its playing characteristics.

PENALTY FOR BREACH OF RULE 5-1 or 5-2: Disqualification.

5-3. Ball Unfit for Play

A ball is unfit for play if it is visibly cut, cracked or out of shape. A ball is not unfit for play solely because mud or other materials adhere to it, its surface is scratched or scraped or its paint is damaged or discolored.

If a player has reason to believe his ball has become unfit for play during play of the hole being played, he may lift the ball, without penalty, to determine whether it is unfit.

Before lifting the ball, the player must announce his intention to his opponent in match play or his *marker* or a *fellow-competitor* in stroke play and mark the position of the ball. He may then lift and examine it, provided that he gives his opponent, *marker* or *fellow-competitor* an opportunity to examine the ball and observe the lifting and replacement. The ball must not be cleaned when lifted under Rule 5-3.

If the player fails to comply with all or any part of this procedure or if he lifts the ball without having reason to believe that it has become unfit for play during play of the hole being played, he incurs a penalty of one stroke.

If it is determined that the ball has become unfit for play during play of the hole being played, the player may *substitute* another ball, placing it on the spot where the original ball lay. Otherwise, the original ball must be replaced. If a player *substitutes* a ball when not permitted and makes a *stroke* at the wrongly *substituted ball*, he incurs the general penalty for a breach of Rule 5-3, but there is no additional penalty under this Rule or Rule 15-2.

If a ball breaks into pieces as a result of a *stroke*, the *stroke* is canceled and the player must play a ball, without penalty, as nearly as possible at the spot from which the original ball was played (see Rule 20-5).

*PENALTY FOR BREACH OF RULE 5-3:
<u>Match play</u> — Loss of hole; <u>Stroke play</u> — Two str[oke]
*If a player incurs the general penalty for breach
there is no additional penalty under this Rule.

Note 1: If the opponent, *marker* or *fellow-competitor* wishes to dispute a claim of unfitness, he must do so before the player plays another ball.

Note 2: If the original lie of a ball to be placed or replaced has been altered, see Rule 20-3b.

(Cleaning ball lifted from putting green or under any other Rule — see Rule 21.)

PLAYER'S RESPONSIBILITIES

Rule 6. The Player

Definitions
All defined terms are in *italics* and are listed alphabetically in the Definitions section — see pages 5-18.

6-1. Rules
The player and his *caddie* are responsible for knowing the *Rules*. During a *stipulated round*, for any breach of a *Rule* by his *caddie*, the player incurs the applicable penalty.

6-2. Handicap

a. Match Play
Before starting a match in a handicap competition, the players should determine from one another their respective handicaps. If a player begins a match having declared a handicap higher than that to which he is entitled and this affects the number of strokes given or received, he is disqualified; otherwise, the player must play off the declared handicap.

b. Stroke Play
In any round of a handicap competition, the *competitor* must ensure that his handicap is recorded on his score card before it is returned to the *Committee*. If no handicap is recorded on his score card before it is returned (Rule 6-6b), or if the recorded

...cap is higher than that to which he is entitled and this ...ects the number of strokes received, he is disqualified from .ne handicap competition; otherwise, the score stands.

Note: It is the player's responsibility to know the holes at which handicap strokes are to be given or received.

6-3. Time of Starting and Groups

a. Time of Starting

The player must start at the time established by the *Committee*.

b. Groups

In stroke play, the *competitor* must remain throughout the round in the group arranged by the *Committee*, unless the *Committee* authorizes or ratifies a change.

PENALTY FOR BREACH OF RULE 6-3: Disqualification.

(Best-ball and four-ball play — see Rules 30-3a and 31-2.)

Note: The *Committee* may provide, in the conditions of a competition (Rule 33-1), that if the player arrives at his starting point, ready to play, within five minutes after his starting time, in the absence of circumstances that warrant waiving the penalty of disqualification as provided in Rule 33-7, the penalty for failure to start on time is loss of the first hole in match play or two strokes at the first hole in stroke play instead of disqualification.

6-4. Caddie

The player may be assisted by a *caddie*, but he is limited to only one *caddie* at any one time.

PENALTY FOR BREACH OF RULE 6-4:

<u>Match play</u> — At the conclusion of the hole at which the breach is discovered, the state of the match is adjusted by deducting one hole for each hole at which a breach occurred; maximum deduction per round — Two holes.

<u>Stroke play</u> — Two strokes for each hole at which any breach occurred; maximum penalty per round — Four strokes.

<u>Match or stroke play</u> — In the event of a breach between the play of two holes, the penalty applies to the next hole.

A player having more than one *caddie* in breach of this Rule must immediately upon the discovery that a breach has occurred ensure that he has no more than one *caddie* at any one time during the remainder of the *stipulated round*. Otherwise, the player is disqualified.

Bogey and par competitions — See Note 1 to Rule 32-1a.

Stableford competitions — See Note 1 to Rule 32-1b.

Note: The *Committee* may, in the conditions of a competition (Rule 33-1), prohibit the use of *caddies* or restrict a player in his choice of *caddie*.

6-5. Ball

The responsibility for playing the proper ball rests with the player. Each player should put an identification mark on his ball.

6-6. Scoring in Stroke Play

a. Recording Scores

After each hole the *marker* should check the score with the *competitor* and record it. On completion of the round, the *marker* must sign the score card and hand it to the *competitor*. If more than one *marker* records the scores, each must sign for the part for which he is responsible.

b. Signing and Returning Score Card

After completion of the round, the *competitor* should check his score for each hole and settle any doubtful points with the *Committee*. He must ensure that the *marker* or *markers* have signed the score card, sign the score card himself and return it to the *Committee* as soon as possible.

PENALTY FOR BREACH OF RULE 6-6b: Disqualification.

c. Alteration of Score Card

No alteration may be made on a score card after the *competitor* has returned it to the *Committee*.

d. Wrong Score for Hole

The *competitor* is responsible for the correctness of the score recorded for each hole on his score card. If he returns a score for any hole lower than actually taken, he is disqualified. If he returns a score for any hole higher than actually taken, the score as returned stands.

Note 1: The *Committee* is responsible for the addition of scores and application of the handicap recorded on the score card — see Rule 33-5.

Note 2: In *four-ball* stroke play, see also Rules 31-3 and 31-7a.

6-7. Undue Delay; Slow Play

The player must play without undue delay and in accordance with any pace of play guidelines that the *Committee* may establish. Between completion of a hole and playing from the next *teeing ground*, the player must not unduly delay play.

PENALTY FOR BREACH OF RULE 6-7:

Match play — Loss of hole; Stroke play — Two strokes.

Bogey and par competitions — See Note 2 to Rule 32-1a.

Stableford competitions — See Note 2 to Rule 32-1b.

For subsequent offense — Disqualification.

Note 1: If the player unduly delays play between holes, he is delaying the play of the next hole and, except for bogey, par and Stableford competitions (see Rule 32), the penalty applies to that hole.

Note 2: For the purpose of preventing slow play, the *Committee* may, in the conditions of a competition (Rule 33-1), establish pace of play guidelines including maximum periods of time allowed to complete a *stipulated round*, a hole or a *stroke*.

In stroke play only, the *Committee* may, in such a condition, modify the penalty for a breach of this Rule as follows:

First offense — One stroke;

Second offense — Two strokes.

For subsequent offense — Disqualification.

6-8. Discontinuance of Play; Resumption of Play

a. When Permitted

The player must not discontinue play unless:

    (i) the *Committee* has suspended play;

    (ii) he believes there is danger from lightning;

    (iii) he is seeking a decision from the *Committee* on a doubtful or disputed point (see Rules 2-5 and 34-3); or

(iv) there is some other good reason such as sudden illness.

Bad weather is not of itself a good reason for discontinuing play.

If the player discontinues play without specific permission from the *Committee*, he must report to the *Committee* as soon as practicable. If he does so and the *Committee* considers his reason satisfactory, there is no penalty. Otherwise, the player is disqualified.

Exception in match play: Players discontinuing match play by agreement are not subject to disqualification, unless by so doing the competition is delayed.

Note: Leaving the *course* does not of itself constitute discontinuance of play.

b. Procedure When Play Suspended by Committee

When play is suspended by the *Committee*, if the players in a match or group are between the play of two holes, they must not resume play until the *Committee* has ordered a resumption of play. If they have started play of a hole, they may discontinue play immediately or continue play of the hole, provided they do so without delay. If the players choose to continue play of the hole, they are permitted to discontinue play before completing it. In any case, play must be discontinued after the hole is completed.

The players must resume play when the *Committee* has ordered a resumption of play.

PENALTY FOR BREACH OF RULE 6-8b: Disqualification.

Note: The *Committee* may provide, in the conditions of a competition (Rule 33-1), that in potentially dangerous situations play must be discontinued immediately following a suspension of play by the *Committee*. If a player fails to discontinue play immediately, he is disqualified, unless circumstances warrant waiving the penalty as provided in Rule 33-7.

c. Lifting Ball When Play Discontinued

When a player discontinues play of a hole under Rule 6-8a, he may lift his ball, without penalty, only if the *Committee* has suspended play or there is a good reason to lift it. Before lifting the ball the player must mark its position. If the player discontinues play and lifts his ball without specific permission from the *Committee*, he must, when reporting to the *Committee* (Rule 6-8a), report the lifting of the ball.

If the player lifts the ball without a good reason to do so, fails to mark the position of the ball before lifting it or fails to report the lifting of the ball, he incurs a penalty of one stroke.

d. Procedure When Play Resumed

Play must be resumed from where it was discontinued, even if resumption occurs on a subsequent day. The player must, either before or when play is resumed, proceed as follows:

(i) if the player has lifted the ball, he must, provided he was entitled to lift it under Rule 6-8c, place the original ball or a *substituted ball* on the spot from which the original ball was lifted. Otherwise, the original ball must be replaced;

(ii) if the player has not lifted his ball, he may, provided he was entitled to lift it under Rule 6-8c, lift, clean and replace the ball, or *substitute* a ball, on the spot from which the original ball was lifted. Before lifting the ball he must mark its position; or

(iii) if the player's ball or ball-marker is moved (including by wind or water) while play is discontinued, a ball or ball-marker must be placed on the spot from which the original ball or ball-marker was moved.

Note: If the spot where the ball is to be placed is impossible to determine, it must be estimated and the ball placed on the estimated spot. The provisions of Rule 20-3c do not apply.

*PENALTY FOR BREACH OF RULE 6-8d:
<u>Match play</u> — Loss of hole; <u>Stroke play</u> — Two strokes.
*If a player incurs the general penalty for a breach of Rule 6-8d, there is no additional penalty under Rule 6-8c.

Rule 7. Practice

Definitions

All defined terms are in *italics* and are listed alphabetically in the Definitions section — see pages 5-18.

7-1. Before or Between Rounds

a. Match Play

On any day of a match-play competition, a player may practice on the competition *course* before a round.

b. Stroke Play

Before a round or play-off on any day of a stroke-play competition, a *competitor* must not practice on the competition *course* or test the surface of any *putting green* on the *course* by rolling a ball or roughening or scraping the surface.

When two or more rounds of a stroke-play competition are to be played over consecutive days, a *competitor* must not practice between those rounds on any competition *course* remaining to be played, or test the surface of any *putting green* on such *course* by rolling a ball or roughening or scraping the surface.

Exception: Practice putting or chipping on or near the first *teeing ground* before starting a round or play-off is permitted.

PENALTY FOR BREACH OF RULE 7-1b: Disqualification.

Note: The *Committee* may, in the conditions of a competition (Rule 33-1), prohibit practice on the competition *course* on any day of a match-play competition or permit practice on the competition *course* or part of the *course* (Rule 33-2c) on any day of or between rounds of a stroke-play competition.

7-2. During Round

A player must not make a practice *stroke* during play of a hole.

Between the play of two holes, a player must not make a practice *stroke,* except that he may practice putting or chipping on or near:

(a) the *putting green* of the hole last played,

(b) any practice *putting green,* or

(c) the *teeing ground* of the next hole to be played in the
    round,

provided a practice *stroke* is not made from a *hazard* and does
not unduly delay play (Rule 6-7).

Strokes made in continuing the play of a hole, the result of
which has been decided, are not practice *strokes*.

Exception: When play has been suspended by the *Committee*,
a player may, prior to resumption of play, practice (a) as provided in this Rule, (b) anywhere other than on the competition
course and (c) as otherwise permitted by the *Committee*.

PENALTY FOR BREACH OF RULE 7-2:
<u>Match play</u> — Loss of hole; <u>Stroke play</u> — Two strokes.
In the event of a breach between the play of two holes, the
penalty applies to the next hole.

Note 1: A practice swing is not a practice *stroke* and may be
taken at any place, provided the player does not breach the
Rules.

Note 2: The *Committee* may, in the conditions of a competition
(Rule 33-1), prohibit:

(a) practice on or near the *putting green* of the hole last
    played, and

(b) rolling a ball on the *putting green* of the hole last
    played.

Rule 8. Advice; Indicating Line of Play

Definitions
All defined terms are in *italics* and are listed alphabetically in
the Definitions section — see pages 5-18.

8-1. Advice

During a *stipulated round*, a player must not:

(a) give *advice* to anyone in the competition playing on the
    course other than his *partner*, or

(b) ask for *advice* from anyone other than his *partner* or
    either of their *caddies*.

8-2. Indicating Line of Play

a. Other Than on Putting Green

Except on the *putting green*, a player may have the *line of play* indicated to him by anyone, but no one may be positioned by the player on or close to the line or an extension of the line beyond the *hole* while the *stroke* is being made. Any mark placed by the player or with his knowledge to indicate the line must be removed before the *stroke* is made.

Exception: *Flagstick* attended or held up — see Rule 17-1.

b. On the Putting Green

When the player's ball is on the *putting green*, the player, his *partner* or either of their *caddies* may, before but not during the *stroke*, point out a line for putting, but in so doing the *putting green* must not be touched. A mark must not be placed anywhere to indicate a line for putting.

PENALTY FOR BREACH OF RULE:

Match play — Loss of hole; Stroke play — Two strokes.

Note: The *Committee* may, in the conditions of a team competition (Rule 33-1), permit each team to appoint one person who may give *advice* (including pointing out a line for putting) to members of that team. The *Committee* may establish conditions relating to the appointment and permitted conduct of that person, who must be identified to the *Committee* before giving *advice*.

Rule 9. Information as to Strokes Taken

Definitions

All defined terms are in *italics* and are listed alphabetically in the Definitions section — see pages 5-18.

9-1. General

The number of *strokes* a player has taken includes any *penalty strokes* incurred.

9-2. Match Play

a. Information as to Strokes Taken

An opponent is entitled to ascertain from the player, during the play of a hole, the number of *strokes* he has taken and, after play of a hole, the number of *strokes* taken on the hole just completed.

b. Wrong Information

A player must not give wrong information to his opponent. If a player gives wrong information, he loses the hole.

A player is deemed to have given wrong information if he:

    (i) fails to inform his opponent as soon as practicable that he has incurred a penalty, unless (a) he was obviously proceeding under a *Rule* involving a penalty and this was observed by his opponent, or (b) he corrects the mistake before his opponent makes his next *stroke*; or

    (ii) gives incorrect information during play of a hole regarding the number of *strokes* taken and does not correct the mistake before his opponent makes his next *stroke;* or

    (iii) gives incorrect information regarding the number of *strokes* taken to complete a hole and this affects the opponent's understanding of the result of the hole, unless he corrects the mistake before any player makes a *stroke* from the next *teeing ground* or, in the case of the last hole of the match, before all players leave the *putting green.*

A player has given wrong information even if it is due to the failure to include a penalty that he did not know he had incurred. It is the player's responsibility to know the *Rules.*

9-3. Stroke Play

A *competitor* who has incurred a penalty should inform his *marker* as soon as practicable.

ORDER OF PLAY

Rule 10. Order of Play

Definitions

All defined terms are in *italics* and are listed alphabetically in the Definitions section — see pages 5-18.

10-1. Match Play

a. When Starting Play of Hole

The *side* that has the *honor* at the first *teeing ground* is determined by the order of the draw. In the absence of a draw, the *honor* should be decided by lot.

The *side* that wins a hole takes the *honor* at the next *teeing ground*. If a hole has been halved, the *side* that had the *honor* at the previous *teeing ground* retains it.

b. During Play of Hole

After both players have started play of the hole, the ball farther from the *hole* is played first. If the balls are equidistant from the *hole* or their positions relative to the *hole* are not determinable, the ball to be played first should be decided by lot.

Exception: Rule 30-3b (*best-ball* and *four-ball* match play).

Note: When it becomes known that the original ball is not to be played as it lies and the player is required to play a ball as nearly as possible at the spot from which the original ball was last played (see Rule 20-5), the order of play is determined by the spot from which the previous *stroke* was made. When a ball may be played from a spot other than where the previous *stroke* was made, the order of play is determined by the position where the original ball came to rest.

c. Playing Out of Turn

If a player plays when his opponent should have played, there is no penalty, but the opponent may immediately require the player to cancel the *stroke* so made and, in correct order, play a ball as nearly as possible at the spot from which the original ball was last played (see Rule 20-5).

10-2. Stroke Play

a. When Starting Play of Hole

The *competitor* who has the *honor* at the first *teeing ground* is determined by the order of the draw. In the absence of a draw, the *honor* should be decided by lot.

The *competitor* with the lowest score at a hole takes the *honor* at the next *teeing ground*. The *competitor* with the second lowest score plays next and so on. If two or more *competitors* have the same score at a hole, they play from the next *teeing ground* in the same order as at the previous *teeing ground*.

Exception: Rule 32-1 (handicap bogey, par and Stableford competitions).

b. During Play of Hole

After the *competitors* have started play of the hole, the ball farthest from the *hole* is played first. If two or more balls are equidistant from the *hole* or their positions relative to the *hole* are not determinable, the ball to be played first should be decided by lot.

Exceptions: Rules 22 (ball assisting or interfering with play) and 31-4 (*four-ball* stroke play).

Note: When it becomes known that the original ball is not to be played as it lies and the *competitor* is required to play a ball as nearly as possible at the spot from which the original ball was last played (see Rule 20-5), the order of play is determined by the spot from which the previous *stroke* was made. When a ball may be played from a spot other than where the previous *stroke* was made, the order of play is determined by the position where the original ball came to rest.

c. Playing Out of Turn

If a *competitor* plays out of turn, there is no penalty and the ball is played as it lies. If, however, the *Committee* determines that *competitors* have agreed to play out of turn to give one of them an advantage, they are disqualified.

(Making stroke while another ball in motion after stroke from putting green — see Rule 16-1f.)

(Incorrect order of play in threesome and foursome stroke play — see Rule 29-3.)

10-3. Provisional Ball or Another Ball from Teeing Ground

If a player plays a *provisional ball* or another ball from the *teeing ground,* he must do so after his opponent or *fellow-competitor* has made his first *stroke*. If more than one player elects to play a *provisional ball* or is required to play another ball from the *teeing ground*, the original order of play must be retained. If a player plays a *provisional ball* or another ball out of turn, Rule 10-1c or 10-2c applies.

TEEING GROUND

Rule 11. Teeing Ground

Definitions
All defined terms are in *italics* and are listed alphabetically in the Definitions section — see pages 5-18.

11-1. Teeing

When a player is putting a ball into play from the *teeing ground*, it must be played from within the *teeing ground* and from the surface of the ground or from a conforming *tee* in or on the surface of the ground.

For the purposes of this Rule, the surface of the ground includes an irregularity of surface (whether or not created by the player) and sand or other natural substance (whether or not placed by the player).

If a player makes a *stroke* at a ball on a non-conforming *tee*, or at a ball teed in a manner not permitted by this Rule, he is disqualified.

A player may stand outside the *teeing ground* to play a ball within it.

11-2. Tee-Markers

Before a player makes his first *stroke* with any ball on the *teeing ground* of the hole being played, the tee-markers are deemed to be fixed. In these circumstances, if the player moves or allows to be moved a tee-marker for the purpose of avoiding interference with his *stance*, the area of his intended swing or his *line of play*, he incurs the penalty for a breach of Rule 13-2.

11-3. Ball Falling off Tee

If a ball, when not *in play*, falls off a *tee* or is knocked off a *tee* by the player in *addressing* it, it may be re-teed, without penalty. However, if a *stroke* is made at the ball in these circumstances, whether the ball is moving or not, the *stroke* counts, but there is no penalty.

11-4. Playing from Outside Teeing Ground

a. Match Play

If a player, when starting a hole, plays a ball from outside the *teeing ground*, there is no penalty, but the opponent may immediately require the player to cancel the *stroke* and play a ball from within the *teeing ground*.

b. Stroke Play

If a *competitor*, when starting a hole, plays a ball from outside the *teeing ground*, he incurs a penalty of two strokes and must then play a ball from within the *teeing ground*.

If the *competitor* makes a *stroke* from the next *teeing ground* without first correcting his mistake or, in the case of the last hole of the round, leaves the *putting green* without first declaring his intention to correct his mistake, he is disqualified.

The *stroke* from outside the *teeing ground* and any subsequent *strokes* by the *competitor* on the hole prior to his correction of the mistake do not count in his score.

11-5. Playing from Wrong Teeing Ground

The provisions of Rule 11-4 apply.

PLAYING THE BALL

Rule 12.
Searching for and Identifying Ball

Definitions

All defined terms are in *italics* and are listed alphabetically in the Definitions section — see pages 5-18.

12-1. Searching for Ball; Seeing Ball

In searching for his ball anywhere on the *course*, the player may touch or bend long grass, rushes, bushes, whins, heather or the like, but only to the extent necessary to find and identify it, provided that this does not improve the lie of the ball, the area of his intended *stance* or swing or his *line of play*.

A player is not necessarily entitled to see his ball when making a *stroke*.

In a *hazard*, if a ball is believed to be covered by *loose impediments* or sand, the player may remove by probing or raking with a club or otherwise, as many *loose impediments* or as much sand as will enable him to see a part of the ball. If an excess is removed, there is no penalty and the ball must be re-covered so that only a part of the ball is visible. If the ball is *moved* during the removal, there is no penalty; the ball must be replaced and, if necessary, re-covered. As to removal of *loose impediments* outside a *hazard*, see Rule 23-1.

If a ball lying in or on an *obstruction* or in an *abnormal ground condition* is accidentally *moved* during search, there is no penalty; the ball must be replaced, unless the player elects to proceed under Rule 24-1b, 24-2b or 25-1b as applicable. If the player replaces the ball, he may still proceed under Rule 24-1b, 24-2b or 25-1b if applicable.

If a ball is believed to be lying in water in a *water hazard*, the player may probe for it with a club or otherwise. If the ball is *moved* in probing, it must be replaced, unless the player elects to proceed under Rule 26-1. There is no penalty for causing the ball to *move*, provided the movement of the ball was directly attributable to the specific act of probing. Otherwise, the player incurs a *penalty stroke* under Rule 18-2a.

PENALTY FOR BREACH OF RULE 12-1:
Match play — Loss of hole; Stroke play — Two strokes.

12-2. Identifying Ball

The responsibility for playing the proper ball rests with the player. Each player should put an identification mark on his ball.

If a player has reason to believe a ball at rest is his and it is necessary to lift the ball in order to identify it, he may lift the ball, without penalty, in order to do so.

Before lifting the ball, the player must announce his intention to his opponent in match play or his *marker* or a *fellow-competitor* in stroke play and mark the position of the ball. He may then lift the ball and identify it, provided that he gives his opponent, *marker* or *fellow-competitor* an opportunity to observe the lifting and replacement. The ball must not be cleaned beyond the extent necessary for identification when lifted under Rule 12-2.

If the ball is the player's ball and he fails to comply with all or any part of this procedure, or he lifts his ball in order to identify it when not necessary to do so, he incurs a penalty of one stroke. If the lifted ball is the player's ball, he must replace it. If he fails to do so, he incurs the general penalty for a breach of Rule 12-2, but there is no additional penalty under this Rule.

Note: If the original lie of a ball to be placed or replaced has been altered, see Rule 20-3b.

*PENALTY FOR BREACH OF RULE 12-2:
Match play — Loss of hole; Stroke play — Two strokes.

*If a player incurs the general penalty for a breach of Rule 12-2, there is no additional penalty under this Rule.

Rule 13. Ball Played as It Lies

Definitions

All defined terms are in *italics* and are listed alphabetically in the Definitions section — see pages 5-18.

13-1. General

The ball must be played as it lies, except as otherwise provided in the *Rules*.

(Ball at rest moved — see Rule 18.)

13-2. Improving Lie, Area of Intended Stance or Swing, or Line of Play

A player must not improve or allow to be improved:

- the position or lie of his ball,
- the area of his intended *stance* or swing,
- his *line of play* or a reasonable extension of that line beyond the *hole*, or
- the area in which he is to drop or place a ball,

by any of the following actions:

- pressing a club on the ground,
- moving, bending or breaking anything growing or fixed (including immovable *obstructions* and objects defining *out of bounds*),
- creating or eliminating irregularities of surface,
- removing or pressing down sand, loose soil, replaced divots or other cut turf placed in position, or
- removing dew, frost or water.

However, the player incurs no penalty if the action occurs:

- in grounding the club lightly when *addressing the ball,*
- in fairly taking his *stance,*
- in making a *stroke* or the backward movement of his club for a *stroke* and the *stroke* is made,

- in creating or eliminating irregularities of surface within the *teeing ground* (Rule 11-1) or in removing dew, frost or water from the *teeing ground*, or

- on the *putting green* in removing sand and loose soil or in repairing damage (Rule 16-1).

Exception: Ball in *hazard* — see Rule 13-4.

13-3. Building Stance

A player is entitled to place his feet firmly in taking his *stance*, but he must not build a *stance*.

13-4. Ball in Hazard; Prohibited Actions

Except as provided in the *Rules*, before making a *stroke* at a ball that is in a *hazard* (whether a *bunker* or a *water hazard*) or that, having been lifted from a *hazard*, may be dropped or placed in the *hazard*, the player must not:

a. Test the condition of the *hazard* or any similar *hazard*;

b. Touch the ground in the *hazard* or water in the *water hazard* with his hand or a club; or

c. Touch or move a *loose impediment* lying in or touching the *hazard*.

Exceptions:

1. Provided nothing is done that constitutes testing the condition of the *hazard* or improves the lie of the ball, there is no penalty if the player (a) touches the ground or *loose impediments* in any *hazard* or water in a *water hazard* as a result of or to prevent falling, in removing an *obstruction*, in measuring or in marking the position of, retrieving, lifting, placing or replacing a ball under any *Rule* or (b) places his clubs in a *hazard*.

2. After making the *stroke,* if the ball is still in the *hazard* or has been lifted from the *hazard* and may be dropped or placed in the *hazard*, the player may smooth sand or soil in the *hazard*, provided nothing is done to breach Rule 13-2 with respect to his next *stroke*. If the ball is outside

the *hazard* after the *stroke*, the player may smooth sand or soil in the *hazard* without restriction.

3. If the player makes a *stroke* from a *hazard* and the ball comes to rest in another *hazard*, Rule 13-4a does not apply to any subsequent actions taken in the *hazard* from which the *stroke* was made.

Note: At any time, including at *address* or in the backward movement for the *stroke*, the player may touch, with a club or otherwise, any *obstruction,* any construction declared by the *Committee* to be an integral part of the *course* or any grass, bush, tree or other growing thing.

PENALTY FOR BREACH OF RULE:
<u>Match play</u> — Loss of hole; <u>Stroke play</u> — Two strokes.

(Searching for ball — see Rule 12-1.)

(Relief for ball in water hazard — see Rule 26.)

Rule 14. Striking the Ball

Definitions
All defined terms are in *italics* and are listed alphabetically in the Definitions section — see pages 5-18.

14-1. Ball to Be Fairly Struck At

The ball must be fairly struck at with the head of the club and must not be pushed, scraped or spooned.

14-2. Assistance

In making a *stroke*, a player must not:

a. Accept physical assistance or protection from the elements; or

b. Allow his *caddie,* his *partner* or his *partner's caddie* to position himself on or close to an extension of the *line of play* or the *line of putt* behind the ball.

PENALTY FOR BREACH OF RULE 14-1 or 14-2:
<u>Match play</u> — Loss of hole; <u>Stroke play</u> — Two strokes.

14-3. Artificial Devices, Unusual Equipment and Unusual Use of Equipment

The United States Golf Association (USGA) reserves the right, at any time, to change the Rules relating to artificial devices, unusual *equipment* and the unusual use of *equipment*, and make or change the interpretations relating to these Rules.

A player in doubt as to whether use of an item would constitute a breach of Rule 14-3 should consult the USGA.

A manufacturer should submit to the USGA a sample of an item to be manufactured for a ruling as to whether its use during a *stipulated round* would cause a player to be in breach of Rule 14-3. The sample becomes the property of the USGA for reference purposes. If a manufacturer fails to submit a sample or, having submitted a sample, fails to await a ruling before manufacturing and/or marketing the item, the manufacturer assumes the risk of a ruling that use of the item would be contrary to the *Rules.*

Except as provided in the *Rules*, during a *stipulated round* the player must not use any artificial device or unusual *equipment*, or use any *equipment* in an unusual manner:

   a. That might assist him in making a *stroke* or in his play; or

   b. For the purpose of gauging or measuring distance or conditions that might affect his play; or

   c. That might assist him in gripping the club, except that:

   (i) plain gloves may be worn;

   (ii) resin, powder and drying or moisturizing agents may be used; and

   (iii) a towel or handkerchief may be wrapped around the grip.

Exceptions:

   1. A player is not in breach of this Rule if (a) the *equipment* or device is designed for or has the effect of alleviating a medical condition, (b) the player has a legitimate medical reason to use the *equipment* or device, and (c) the *Committee* is satisfied that its use does not give the player any undue advantage over other players.

2. A player is not in breach of this Rule if he uses *equipment* in a traditionally accepted manner.

PENALTY FOR BREACH OF RULE 14-3: Disqualification.

Note: The *Committee* may make a Local Rule allowing players to use devices that measure or gauge distance only.

14-4. Striking the Ball More Than Once

If a player's club strikes the ball more than once in the course of a *stroke*, the player must count the *stroke* and add a *penalty stroke*, making two *strokes* in all.

14-5. Playing Moving Ball

A player must not make a *stroke* at his ball while it is moving.

Exceptions:

- Ball falling off *tee* — Rule 11-3.
- Striking the ball more than once — Rule 14-4.
- Ball moving in water — Rule 14-6.

When the ball begins to *move* only after the player has begun the *stroke* or the backward movement of his club for the *stroke*, he incurs no penalty under this Rule for playing a moving ball, but he is not exempt from any penalty under the following Rules:

- Ball at rest *moved* by player — Rule 18-2a.
- Ball at rest moving after *address* — Rule 18-2b.

(Ball purposely deflected or stopped by player, partner or caddie — see Rule 1-2.)

14-6. Ball Moving in Water

When a ball is moving in water in a *water hazard*, the player may, without penalty, make a *stroke*, but he must not delay making his *stroke* in order to allow the wind or current to improve the position of the ball. A ball moving in water in a *water hazard* may be lifted if the player elects to invoke Rule 26.

PENALTY FOR BREACH OF RULE 14-5 or 14-6:
<u>Match play</u> — Loss of hole; <u>Stroke play</u> — Two strokes.

Rule 15. Substituted Ball; Wrong Ball

Definitions

All defined terms are in *italics* and are listed alphabetically in the Definitions section — see pages 5-18.

15-1. General

A player must *hole* out with the ball played from the *teeing ground* unless the ball is *lost* or *out of bounds* or the player *substitutes* another ball, whether or not substitution is permitted (see Rule 15-2). If a player plays a *wrong ball*, see Rule 15-3.

15-2. Substituted Ball

A player may *substitute* a ball when proceeding under a *Rule* that permits the player to play, drop or place another ball in completing the play of a hole. The *substituted ball* becomes the *ball in play*.

If a player *substitutes* a ball when not permitted to do so under the *Rules*, that *substituted ball* is not a *wrong ball*; it becomes the *ball in play*. If the mistake is not corrected as provided in Rule 20-6 and the player makes a *stroke* at a wrongly *substituted ball*, he loses the hole in match play or incurs a penalty of two strokes in stroke play under the applicable *Rule* and, in stroke play, must play out the hole with the *substituted ball*.

Exception: If a player incurs a penalty for making a *stroke* from a wrong place, there is no additional penalty for substituting a ball when not permitted.

(Playing from wrong place — see Rule 20-7.)

15-3. Wrong Ball

a. Match Play

If a player makes a *stroke* at a *wrong ball*, he loses the hole.

If the *wrong ball* belongs to another player, its owner must place a ball on the spot from which the *wrong ball* was first played.

If the player and opponent exchange balls during the play of a hole, the first to make a *stroke* at a *wrong ball* loses the hole;

when this cannot be determined, the hole must be played out with the balls exchanged.

Exception: There is no penalty if a player makes a *stroke* at a *wrong ball* that is moving in water in a *water hazard*. Any *strokes* made at a *wrong ball* moving in water in a *water hazard* do not count in the player's score. The player must correct his mistake by playing the correct ball or by proceeding under the *Rules*.

b. Stroke Play

If a *competitor* makes a *stroke* or *strokes* at a *wrong ball*, he incurs a penalty of two strokes.

The *competitor* must correct his mistake by playing the correct ball or by proceeding under the *Rules*. If he fails to correct his mistake before making a *stroke* on the next *teeing ground* or, in the case of the last hole of the round, fails to declare his intention to correct his mistake before leaving the *putting green*, he is disqualified.

Strokes made by a *competitor* with a *wrong ball* do not count in his score. If the *wrong ball* belongs to another *competitor*, its owner must place a ball on the spot from which the *wrong ball* was first played.

Exception: There is no penalty if a *competitor* makes a *stroke* at a *wrong ball* that is moving in water in a *water hazard*. Any *strokes* made at a *wrong ball* moving in water in a *water hazard* do not count in the *competitor's* score.

(Lie of ball to be placed or replaced altered — see Rule 20-3b.)

(Spot not determinable — see Rule 20-3c.)

Rule 16. The Putting Green

Definitions

All defined terms are in *italics* and are listed alphabetically in the Definitions section — see pages 5-18.

16-1. General

a. Touching Line of Putt

The *line of putt* must not be touched except:

    (i) the player may remove *loose impediments*, provided he does not press anything down;

    (ii) the player may place the club in front of the ball when *addressing* it, provided he does not press anything down;

    (iii) in measuring — Rule 18-6;

    (iv) in lifting or replacing the ball — Rule 16-1b;

    (v) in pressing down a ball-marker;

    (vi) in repairing old *hole* plugs or ball marks on the *putting green* — Rule 16-1c; and

    (vii) in removing movable *obstructions* — Rule 24-1.

(Indicating line for putting on putting green — see Rule 8-2b.)

b. Lifting and Cleaning Ball

A ball on the *putting green* may be lifted and, if desired, cleaned. The position of the ball must be marked before it is lifted, and the ball must be replaced (see Rule 20-1).

c. Repair of Hole Plugs, Ball Marks and Other Damage

The player may repair an old *hole* plug or damage to the *putting green* caused by the impact of a ball, whether or not the player's ball lies on the *putting green*. If a ball or ball-marker is accidentally *moved* in the process of the repair, the ball or ball-marker must be replaced. There is no penalty, provided the movement of the ball or ball-marker is directly attributable to the specific act of repairing an old *hole* plug or damage to the *putting green* caused by the impact of a ball. Otherwise, Rule 18 applies.

Any other damage to the *putting green* must not be repaired if it might assist the player in his subsequent play of the hole.

d. Testing Surface

During the *stipulated round*, a player must not test the surface of any *putting green* by rolling a ball or roughening or scraping the surface.

Exception: Between the play of two holes, a player may test the surface of any practice *putting green* and the *putting green* of the hole last played, unless the *Committee* has prohibited such action (see Note 2 to Rule 7-2).

e. Standing Astride or on Line of Putt

The player must not make a *stroke* on the *putting green* from a *stance* astride, or with either foot touching, the *line of putt* or an extension of that line behind the ball.

Exception: There is no penalty if the *stance* is inadvertently taken on or astride the *line of putt* (or an extension of that line behind the ball) or is taken to avoid standing on another player's *line of putt* or prospective *line of putt*.

f. Making Stroke While Another Ball in Motion

The player must not make a *stroke* while another ball is in motion after a *stroke* from the *putting green*, except that if a player does so, there is no penalty if it was his turn to play.

(Lifting ball assisting or interfering with play while another ball in motion — see Rule 22.)

PENALTY FOR BREACH OF RULE 16-1:

<u>Match play</u> — Loss of hole; <u>Stroke play</u> — Two strokes.

(Position of caddie or partner — see Rule 14-2.)

(Wrong putting green — see Rule 25-3.)

16-2. Ball Overhanging Hole

When any part of the ball overhangs the lip of the *hole*, the player is allowed enough time to reach the *hole* without unreasonable delay and an additional ten seconds to determine whether the ball is at rest. If by then the ball has not fallen into the *hole*, it is deemed to be at rest. If the ball subsequently falls into the *hole*, the player is deemed to have *holed* out with his last *stroke* and must add a *penalty stroke* to his score for the hole; otherwise, there is no penalty under this Rule.

(Undue delay — see Rule 6-7.)

Rule 17. The Flagstick

Definitions

All defined terms are in *italics* and are listed alphabetically in the Definitions section — see pages 5-18.

17-1. Flagstick Attended, Removed or Held Up

Before making a *stroke* from anywhere on the *course*, the player may have the *flagstick* attended, removed or held up to indicate the position of the *hole*.

If the *flagstick* is not attended, removed or held up before the player makes a *stroke*, it must not be attended, removed or held up during the *stroke* or while the player's ball is in motion if doing so might influence the movement of the ball.

Note 1: If the *flagstick* is in the *hole* and anyone stands near it while a *stroke* is being made, he is deemed to be attending the *flagstick*.

Note 2: If, prior to the *stroke*, the *flagstick* is attended, removed or held up by anyone with the player's knowledge and he makes no objection, the player is deemed to have authorized it.

Note 3: If anyone attends or holds up the *flagstick* while a *stroke* is being made, he is deemed to be attending the *flagstick* until the ball comes to rest.

(Moving attended, removed or held up flagstick while ball in motion — see Rule 24-1.)

17-2. Unauthorized Attendance

If an opponent or his *caddie* in match play or a *fellow-competitor* or his *caddie* in stroke play, without the player's authority or prior knowledge, attends, removes or holds up the *flagstick* during the *stroke* or while the ball is in motion, and the act might influence the movement of the ball, the opponent or *fellow-competitor* incurs the applicable penalty.

PENALTY FOR BREACH OF RULE 17-1 or 17-2:
Match play — Loss of hole; Stroke play — Two strokes.

In stroke play, if a breach of Rule 17-2 occurs and the *competitor's* ball subsequently strikes the *flagstick,* the person attending or holding it or anything carried by him, the *competitor* incurs no penalty. The ball is played as it lies, except that if the *stroke* was made on the *putting green,* the *stroke* is canceled and the ball must be replaced and replayed.

17-3. Ball Striking Flagstick or Attendant

The player's ball must not strike:

a. The *flagstick* when it is attended, removed or held up;

b. The person attending or holding up the *flagstick* or anything carried by him; or

c. The *flagstick* in the *hole,* unattended, when the *stroke* has been made on the *putting green.*

Exception: When the *flagstick* is attended, removed or held up without the player's authority — see Rule 17-2.

PENALTY FOR BREACH OF RULE 17-3:
Match play — Loss of hole; Stroke play — Two strokes and the ball must be played as it lies.

17-4. Ball Resting Against Flagstick

When a player's ball rests against the *flagstick* in the *hole* and the ball is not *holed,* the player or another person authorized by him may move or remove the *flagstick,* and if the ball falls into the *hole,* the player is deemed to have *holed* out with his last *stroke;* otherwise, the ball, if *moved,* must be placed on the lip of the *hole,* without penalty.

Rule 18. Ball at Rest Moved

Definitions

All defined terms are in *italics* and are listed alphabetically in the Definitions section — see pages 5-18.

18-1. By Outside Agency

If a ball at rest is *moved* by an *outside agency*, there is no penalty and the ball must be replaced.

Note: It is a question of fact whether a ball has been *moved* by an *outside agency*. In order to apply this Rule, it must be known or virtually certain that an *outside agency* has *moved* the ball. In the absence of such knowledge or certainty, the player must play the ball as it lies or, if the ball is not found, proceed under Rule 27-1.

(Player's ball at rest moved by another ball — see Rule 18-5.)

18-2. By Player, Partner, Caddie or Equipment

a. General

When a player's ball is *in play*, if:

    (i) the player, his *partner* or either of their *caddies* lifts or *moves* it, touches it purposely (except with a club in the act of *addressing* it) or causes it to *move* except as permitted by a *Rule*, or

    (ii) *equipment* of the player or his *partner* causes the ball to *move*

the player incurs a penalty of one stroke. If the ball is moved, it must be replaced, unless the movement of the ball occurs after the player has begun the *stroke* or the backward movement of the club for the *stroke* and the *stroke* is made.

Under the *Rules* there is no penalty if a player accidentally causes his ball to *move* in the following circumstances:

- In searching for a ball in a *hazard* covered by *loose impediments* or sand, for a ball in an *obstruction* or *abnormal ground condition* or for a ball believed to be in water in a *water hazard* — Rule 12-1

- In repairing a *hole* plug or ball mark — Rule 16-1c
- In measuring — Rule 18-6
- In lifting a ball under a *Rule* — Rule 20-1
- In placing or replacing a ball under a *Rule* — Rule 20-3a
- In removing a *loose impediment* on the *putting green* — Rule 23-1
- In removing movable *obstructions* — Rule 24-1.

b. Ball Moving After Address

If a player's *ball in play moves* after he has *addressed* it (other than as a result of a *stroke*), the player is deemed to have *moved* the ball and incurs a penalty of one stroke. The ball must be replaced, unless the movement of the ball occurs after the player has begun the *stroke* or the backward movement of the club for the *stroke* and the *stroke* is made.

18-3. By Opponent, Caddie or Equipment in Match Play

a. During Search

If, during search for a player's ball, an opponent, his *caddie* or his *equipment moves* the ball, touches it or causes it to *move*, there is no penalty. If the ball is *moved*, it must be replaced.

b. Other Than During Search

If, other than during search for a player's ball, an opponent, his *caddie* or his *equipment moves* the ball, touches it purposely or causes it to *move*, except as otherwise provided in the *Rules*, the opponent incurs a penalty of one stroke. If the ball is *moved*, it must be replaced.

(Playing a wrong ball — see Rule 15-3.)

(Ball moved in measuring — see Rule 18-6.)

18-4. By Fellow-Competitor, Caddie or Equipment in Stroke Play

If a *fellow-competitor*, his *caddie* or his *equipment moves* the player's ball, touches it or causes it to *move*, there is no penalty. If the ball is *moved*, it must be replaced.

(Playing a wrong ball — see Rule 15-3.)

18-5. By Another Ball

If a *ball in play* and at rest is *moved* by another ball in motion after a *stroke*, the *moved* ball must be replaced.

18-6. Ball Moved in Measuring

If a ball or ball-marker is *moved* in measuring while proceeding under or in determining the application of a *Rule,* the ball or ball-marker must be replaced. There is no penalty, provided the movement of the ball or ball-marker is directly attributable to the specific act of measuring. Otherwise, the provisions of Rule 18-2a, 18-3b or 18-4 apply.

*PENALTY FOR BREACH OF RULE:
<u>Match play</u> — Loss of hole; <u>Stroke play</u> — Two strokes.
*If a player who is required to replace a ball fails to do so, or if he makes a *stroke* at a ball *substituted* under Rule 18 when such *substitution* is not permitted, he incurs the general penalty for breach of Rule 18, but there is no additional penalty under this Rule.

Note 1: If a ball to be replaced under this Rule is not immediately recoverable, another ball may be *substituted*.

Note 2: If the original lie of a ball to be placed or replaced has been altered, see Rule 20-3b.

Note 3: If it is impossible to determine the spot on which a ball is to be placed, see Rule 20-3c.

Rule 19. Ball in Motion Deflected or Stopped

Definitions
All defined terms are in *italics* and are listed alphabetically in the Definitions section — see pages 5-18.

19-1. By Outside Agency

If a player's ball in motion is accidentally deflected or stopped by any *outside agency,* it is a *rub of the green,* there is no penalty and the ball must be played as it lies, except:

    a. If a player's ball in motion after a *stroke* other than on the *putting green* comes to rest in or on any moving or animate *outside agency*, the ball must *through the green* or in a *hazard* be dropped, or on the *putting green* be placed, as near as possible to the spot directly under the place where the ball came to rest in or on the *outside agency*, but not nearer the *hole*, and

b. If a player's ball in motion after a *stroke* on the *putting green* is deflected or stopped by, or comes to rest in or on, any moving or animate *outside agency*, except a worm, insect or the like, the *stroke* is canceled. The ball must be replaced and replayed.

If the ball is not immediately recoverable, another ball may be *substituted*.

Exception: Ball striking person attending or holding up *flagstick* or anything carried by him — see Rule 17-3b.

Note: If the *referee* or the *Committee* determines that a player's ball has been purposely deflected or stopped by an *outside agency*, Rule 1-4 applies to the player. If the *outside agency* is a *fellow-competitor* or his *caddie*, Rule 1-2 applies to the *fellow-competitor*.

(Player's ball deflected or stopped by another ball — see Rule 19-5.)

19-2. By Player, Partner, Caddie or Equipment

If a player's ball is accidentally deflected or stopped by himself, his *partner* or either of their *caddies* or *equipment*, the player incurs a penalty of one stroke. The ball must be played as it lies, except when it comes to rest in or on the player's, his *partner's* or either of their *caddies'* clothes or *equipment*, in which case the ball must *through the green* or in a *hazard* be dropped, or on the *putting green* be placed, as near as possible to the spot directly under the place where the ball came to rest in or on the article, but not nearer the *hole*.

Exception 1: Ball striking person attending or holding up *flagstick* or anything carried by him — see Rule 17-3b.

Exception 2: Dropped ball — see Rule 20-2a.

(Ball purposely deflected or stopped by player, partner or caddie — see Rule 1-2.)

19-3. By Opponent, Caddie or Equipment in Match Play

If a player's ball is accidentally deflected or stopped by an opponent, his *caddie* or his *equipment*, there is no penalty. The player may, before another *stroke* is made by either *side*, cancel the *stroke* and play a ball, without penalty, as nearly as possible at the spot from which the original ball was last played (see Rule 20-5) or he may play the ball as it lies. However, if the player elects not to cancel the *stroke* and the ball has come to rest in or on the opponent's or his *caddie*'s clothes or *equipment*, the ball must *through the green* or in a *hazard* be dropped, or on the *putting green* be placed, as near as possible to the spot directly under the place where the ball came to rest in or on the article, but not nearer the *hole*.

Exception: Ball striking person attending or holding up *flagstick* or anything carried by him — see Rule 17-3b.

(Ball purposely deflected or stopped by opponent or caddie — see Rule 1-2.)

19-4. By Fellow-Competitor, Caddie or Equipment in Stroke Play

See Rule 19-1 regarding ball deflected by *outside agency*.

Exception: Ball striking person attending or holding up *flagstick* or anything carried by him — see Rule 17-3b.

19-5. By Another Ball

a. At Rest

If a player's ball in motion after a *stroke* is deflected or stopped by a *ball in play* and at rest, the player must play his ball as it lies. In match play, there is no penalty. In stroke play, there is no penalty, unless both balls lay on the *putting green* prior to the *stroke*, in which case the player incurs a penalty of two strokes.

b. In Motion

If a player's ball in motion after a *stroke* is deflected or stopped by another ball in motion after a *stroke*, the player must play his ball as it lies. There is no penalty, unless the player was in breach of Rule 16-1f, in which case he incurs the penalty for breach of that Rule.

Exception: If the player's ball is in motion aft putting green and the other ball in motion is a — see Rule 19-1b.

PENALTY FOR BREACH OF RULE:
<u>Match play</u> — Loss of hole; <u>Stroke play</u> — Two str

---

RELIEF SITUATIONS AND PROCEDURE

Rule 20. Lifting, Dropping and Placing; Playing from Wrong Place

Definitions
All defined terms are in *italics* and are listed alphabetically in the Definitions section — see pages 5-18.

20-1. Lifting and Marking

A ball to be lifted under the *Rules* may be lifted by the player, his *partner* or another person authorized by the player. In any such case, the player is responsible for any breach of the *Rules*.

The position of the ball must be marked before it is lifted under a *Rule* that requires it to be replaced. If it is not marked, the player incurs a penalty of one stroke and the ball must be replaced. If it is not replaced, the player incurs the general penalty for breach of this Rule, but there is no additional penalty under Rule 20-1.

If a ball or ball-marker is accidentally *moved* in the process of lifting the ball under a *Rule* or marking its position, the ball or ball-marker must be replaced. There is no penalty, provided the movement of the ball or ball-marker is directly attributable to the specific act of marking the position of or lifting the ball. Otherwise, the player incurs a penalty of one stroke under this Rule or Rule 18-2a.

Exception: If a player incurs a penalty for failing to act in accordance with Rule 5-3 or 12-2, there is no additional penalty under Rule 20-1.

Note: The position of a ball to be lifted should be marked by

ball-marker, a small coin or other similar object
~~~~ately behind the ball. If the ball-marker interferes with
play, *stance* or *stroke* of another player, it should be placed
one or more clubhead-lengths to one side.

20-2. Dropping and Re-Dropping

a. By Whom and How

A ball to be dropped under the *Rules* must be dropped by the
player himself. He must stand erect, hold the ball at shoulder
height and arm's length and drop it. If a ball is dropped by any
other person or in any other manner and the error is not corrected as provided in Rule 20-6, the player incurs a penalty of
one stroke.

If the ball when dropped touches any person or the *equipment*
of any player before or after it strikes a part of the *course* and
before it comes to rest, the ball must be re-dropped, without
penalty. There is no limit to the number of times a ball must
be re-dropped in these circumstances.

(Taking action to influence position or movement of ball — see
Rule 1-2.)

b. Where to Drop

When a ball is to be dropped as near as possible to a specific
spot, it must be dropped not nearer the *hole* than the specific
spot which, if it is not precisely known to the player, must be
estimated.

A ball when dropped must first strike a part of the *course* where
the applicable *Rule* requires it to be dropped. If it is not so
dropped, Rules 20-6 and 20-7 apply.

c. When to Re-Drop

A dropped ball must be re-dropped, without penalty, if it:

  (i) rolls into and comes to rest in a *hazard*;

  (ii) rolls out of and comes to rest outside a *hazard*;

  (iii) rolls onto and comes to rest on a *putting green*;

  (iv) rolls and comes to rest *out of bounds*;

  (v) rolls to and comes to rest in a position where there is

interference by the condition from which relief was taken under Rule 24-2b (immovable obstruction), Rule 25-1 (abnormal ground conditions), Rule 25-3 (wrong putting green) or a Local Rule (Rule 33-8a), or rolls back into the pitch-mark from which it was lifted under Rule 25-2 (embedded ball);

(vi) rolls and comes to rest more than two club-lengths from where it first struck a part of the *course*; or

(vii) rolls and comes to rest nearer the *hole* than:

(a) its original position or estimated position (see Rule 20-2b) unless otherwise permitted by the *Rules*; or

(b) the *nearest point of relief* or maximum available relief (Rule 24-2, 25-1 or 25-3); or

(c) the point where the original ball last crossed the margin of the *water hazard* or *lateral water hazard* (Rule 26-1).

If the ball when re-dropped rolls into any position listed above, it must be placed as near as possible to the spot where it first struck a part of the *course* when re-dropped.

Note 1: If a ball when dropped or re-dropped comes to rest and subsequently *moves*, the ball must be played as it lies, unless the provisions of any other *Rule* apply.

Note 2: If a ball to be re-dropped or placed under this Rule is not immediately recoverable, another ball may be *substituted*.

(Use of Dropping Zone — see Appendix I; Part B; Section 8.)

20-3. Placing and Replacing

a. By Whom and Where

A ball to be placed under the *Rules* must be placed by the player or his *partner*. If a ball is to be replaced, the player, his *partner* or the person who lifted or *moved* it must place it on the spot from which it was lifted or *moved*. If the ball is placed or replaced by any other person and the error is not corrected as provided in Rule 20-6, the player incurs a penalty of one stroke. In any such case, the player is responsible for any other breach of the *Rules* that occurs as a result of the placing or replacing of the ball.

If a ball or ball-marker is accidentally *moved* in the process of placing or replacing the ball, the ball or ball-marker must be replaced. There is no penalty, provided the movement of the ball or ball-marker is directly attributable to the specific act of placing or replacing the ball or removing the ball-marker. Otherwise, the player incurs a penalty of one stroke under Rule 18-2a or 20-1.

If a ball to be replaced is placed other than on the spot from which it was lifted or *moved* and the error is not corrected as provided in Rule 20-6, the player incurs the general penalty, loss of hole in match play or two strokes in stroke play, for a breach of the applicable *Rule*.

b. Lie of Ball to Be Placed or Replaced Altered

If the original lie of a ball to be placed or replaced has been altered:

   (i) except in a *hazard*, the ball must be placed in the nearest lie most similar to the original lie that is not more than one club-length from the original lie, not nearer the *hole* and not in a *hazard*;

   (ii) in a *water hazard*, the ball must be placed in accordance with Clause (i) above, except that the ball must be placed in the *water hazard*;

   (iii) in a *bunker*, the original lie must be re-created as nearly as possible and the ball must be placed in that lie.

c. Spot Not Determinable

If it is impossible to determine the spot where the ball is to be placed or replaced:

   (i) *through the green*, the ball must be dropped as near as possible to the place where it lay but not in a *hazard* or on a *putting green;*

   (ii) in a *hazard*, the ball must be dropped in the *hazard* as near as possible to the place where it lay;

   (iii) on the *putting green*, the ball must be placed as near as possible to the place where it lay but not in a *hazard*.

Exception: When resuming play (Rule 6-8d), if the spot where the ball is to be placed is impossible to determine, it must be estimated and the ball placed on the estimated spot.

d. Ball Fails to Come to Rest on Spot

If a ball when placed fails to come to rest on the spot on which it was placed, there is no penalty and the ball must be replaced. If it still fails to come to rest on that spot:

(i) except in a *hazard*, it must be placed at the nearest spot where it can be placed at rest that is not nearer the *hole* and not in a *hazard*;

(ii) in a *hazard*, it must be placed in the *hazard* at the nearest spot where it can be placed at rest that is not nearer the *hole*.

If a ball when placed comes to rest on the spot on which it is placed, and it subsequently *moves*, there is no penalty and the ball must be played as it lies, unless the provisions of any other *Rule* apply.

PENALTY FOR BREACH OF RULE 20-1, 20-2 or 20-3:
Match play — Loss of hole; Stroke play — Two strokes.

20-4. When Ball Dropped or Placed Is in Play

If the player's *ball in play* has been lifted, it is again in play when dropped or placed.

A *substituted ball* becomes the *ball in play* when it has been dropped or placed.

(Ball incorrectly substituted — see Rule 15-2.)

(Lifting ball incorrectly substituted, dropped or placed — see Rule 20-6.)

20-5. Making Next Stroke from Where Previous Stroke Made

When a player elects or is required to make his next *stroke* from where a previous *stroke* was made, he must proceed as follows:

a. On the Teeing Ground: The ball to be played must be played from within the *teeing ground*. It may be played from anywhere within the *teeing ground* and may be teed.

b. Through the Green: The ball to be played must be dropped and when dropped must first strike a part of the *course through the green*.

c. In a Hazard: The ball to be played must be dropped and when dropped must first strike a part of the *course* in the *hazard*.

d. On the Putting Green: The ball to be played must be placed on the *putting green*.

PENALTY FOR BREACH OF RULE 20-5:
<u>Match play</u> — Loss of hole; <u>Stroke play</u> — Two strokes.

20-6. Lifting Ball Incorrectly Substituted, Dropped or Placed

A ball incorrectly *substituted,* dropped or placed in a wrong place or otherwise not in accordance with the *Rules* but not played may be lifted, without penalty, and the player must then proceed correctly.

20-7. Playing from Wrong Place

a. General

A player has played from a wrong place if he makes a *stroke* at his *ball in play:*

(i) on a part of the *course* where the *Rules* do not permit a *stroke* to be played or a ball to be dropped or placed; or

(ii) when the *Rules* require a dropped ball to be re-dropped or a *moved* ball to be replaced.

Note: For a ball played from outside the *teeing ground* or from a wrong *teeing ground* — see Rule 11-4.

b. Match Play

If a player makes a *stroke* from a wrong place, he loses the hole.

c. Stroke Play

If a *competitor* makes a *stroke* from a wrong place, he incurs a penalty of two strokes under the applicable *Rule*. He must play out the hole with the ball played from the wrong place, without correcting his error, provided he has not committed a serious breach (see Note 1).

If a *competitor* becomes aware that he has played from a wrong place and believes that he may have committed a serious breach, he must, before making a *stroke* on the next *teeing ground,* play out the hole with a second ball played in accordance with the *Rules.* If the hole being played is the last hole of the round, he must declare, before leaving the *putting green,* that he will play out the hole with a second ball played in accordance with the *Rules.*

If the *competitor* has played a second ball, he must report the facts to the *Committee* before returning his score card; if he fails to do so, he is disqualified. The *Committee* must determine whether the *competitor* has committed a serious breach of the applicable *Rule.* If he has, the score with the second ball counts and the *competitor* must add two *penalty strokes* to his score with that ball. If the *competitor* has committed a serious breach and has failed to correct it as outlined above, he is disqualified.

Note 1: A *competitor* is deemed to have committed a serious breach of the applicable *Rule* if the *Committee* considers he has gained a significant advantage as a result of playing from a wrong place.

Note 2: If a *competitor* plays a second ball under Rule 20-7c and it is ruled not to count, *strokes* made with that ball and *penalty strokes* incurred solely by playing that ball are disregarded. If the second ball is ruled to count, the *stroke* made from the wrong place and any *strokes* subsequently taken with the original ball including *penalty strokes* incurred solely by playing that ball are disregarded.

Note 3: If a player incurs a penalty for making a *stroke* from a wrong place, there is no additional penalty for *substituting* a ball when not permitted.

Rule 21. Cleaning Ball

Definitions

All defined terms are in *italics* and are listed alphabetically in the Definitions section — see pages 5-18.

A ball on the *putting green* may be cleaned when lifted under Rule 16-1b. Elsewhere, a ball may be cleaned when lifted, except when it has been lifted:

a. To determine if it is unfit for play (Rule 5-3);

b. For identification (Rule 12-2), in which case it may be cleaned only to the extent necessary for identification; or

c. Because it is assisting or interfering with play (Rule 22).

If a player cleans his ball during play of a hole except as provided in this Rule, he incurs a penalty of one stroke and the ball, if lifted, must be replaced.

If a player who is required to replace a ball fails to do so, he incurs the general penalty under the applicable *Rule*, but there is no additional penalty under Rule 21.

Exception: If a player incurs a penalty for failing to act in accordance with Rule 5-3, 12-2 or 22, there is no additional penalty under Rule 21.

Rule 22.
Ball Assisting or Interfering with Play

Definitions

All defined terms are in *italics* and are listed alphabetically in the Definitions section — see pages 5-18.

22-1. Ball Assisting Play

Except when a ball is in motion, if a player considers that a ball might assist any other player, he may:

a. Lift the ball if it is his ball, or

b. Have any other ball lifted.

A ball lifted under this Rule must be replaced (see Rule 20-3). The ball must not be cleaned, unless it lies on the *putting green* (see Rule 21).

In stroke play, a player required to lift his ball may play first rather than lift the ball.

In stroke play, if the *Committee* determines that *competitors* have agreed not to lift a ball that might assist any *competitor*, they are disqualified.

22-2. Ball Interfering with Play

Except when a ball is in motion, if a player considers that another ball might interfere with his play, he may have it lifted.

A ball lifted under this Rule must be replaced (see Rule 20-3). The ball must not be cleaned, unless it lies on the *putting green* (see Rule 21).

In stroke play, a player required to lift his ball may play first rather than lift the ball.

Note: Except on the *putting green,* a player may not lift his ball solely because he considers that it might interfere with the play of another player. If a player lifts his ball without being asked to do so, he incurs a penalty of one stroke for a breach of Rule 18-2a, but there is no additional penalty under Rule 22.

PENALTY FOR BREACH OF RULE:
<u>Match play</u> — Loss of hole; <u>Stroke play</u> — Two strokes.

Rule 23. Loose Impediments

Definitions

All defined terms are in *italics* and are listed alphabetically in the Definitions section — see pages 5-18.

23-1. Relief

Except when both the *loose impediment* and the ball lie in or touch the same *hazard*, any *loose impediment* may be removed without penalty.

If the ball lies anywhere other than on the *putting green* and the removal of a *loose impediment* by the player causes the ball to *move,* Rule 18-2a applies.

On the *putting green,* if the ball or ball-marker is accidentally *moved* in the process of removing a *loose impediment,* the ball or ball-marker must be replaced. There is no penalty, provided the movement of the ball or ball-marker is directly attributable to the removal of the *loose impediment.* Otherwise, if the player causes the ball to *move,* he incurs a penalty of one stroke under Rule 18-2a.

When a ball is in motion, a *loose impediment* that might influence the movement of the ball must not be removed.

Note: If the ball lies in a *hazard,* the player must not touch or move any *loose impediment* lying in or touching the same *hazard* — see Rule 13-4c.

PENALTY FOR BREACH OF RULE:
<u>Match play</u> — Loss of hole; <u>Stroke play</u> — Two strokes.

(Searching for ball in hazard — see Rule 12-1.)

(Touching line of putt — see Rule 16-1a.)

Rule 24. Obstructions

Definitions
All defined terms are in *italics* and are listed alphabetically in the Definitions section — see pages 5-18.

24-1. Movable Obstruction

A player may take relief, without penalty, from a movable *obstruction* as follows:

a. If the ball does not lie in or on the *obstruction,* the *obstruction* may be removed. If the ball *moves,* it must be replaced, and there is no penalty, provided that the movement of the ball is directly attributable to the removal of the *obstruction.* Otherwise, Rule 18-2a applies.

b. If the ball lies in or on the *obstruction,* the ball may be lifted and the *obstruction* removed. The ball must *through the green* or in a *hazard* be dropped, or on the *putting green* be placed, as near as possible to the spot directly under the place where the ball lay in or on the *obstruction*, but not nearer the *hole*.

The ball may be cleaned when lifted under this Rule.

When a ball is in motion, an *obstruction* that might influence the movement of the ball, other than *equipment* of any player or the *flagstick* when attended, removed or held up, must not be moved.

(Exerting influence on ball — see Rule 1-2.)

Note: If a ball to be dropped or placed under this Rule is not immediately recoverable, another ball may be *substituted*.

24-2. Immovable Obstruction

a. Interference

Interference by an immovable *obstruction* occurs when a ball lies in or on the *obstruction*, or when the *obstruction* interferes with the player's *stance* or the area of his intended swing. If the player's ball lies on the *putting green,* interference also occurs if an immovable *obstruction* on the *putting green* intervenes on his *line of putt*. Otherwise, intervention on the *line of play* is not, of itself, interference under this Rule.

b. Relief

Except when the ball is in a *water hazard* or a *lateral water hazard*, a player may take relief from interference by an immovable *obstruction* as follows:

(i) Through the Green: If the ball lies *through the green*, the player must lift the ball and drop it, without penalty, within one club-length of and not nearer the *hole* than the *nearest point of relief*. The *nearest point of relief* must not be in a *hazard* or on a *putting green*. When the ball is dropped within one club-length of the *nearest point of relief,* the ball must first strike a part of the *course* at a spot that avoids interference by the immovable *obstruction* and is not in a *hazard* and not on a *putting green*.

(ii) In a Bunker: If the ball is in a *bunker*, the player must
lift the ball and drop it either:

(a) Without penalty, in accordance with Clause (i) above,
except that the *nearest point of relief* must be in the *bunker* and the ball must be dropped in the *bunker;* or

(b) Under penalty of one stroke, outside the *bunker* keeping the point where the ball lay directly between the
hole and the spot on which the ball is dropped, with
no limit to how far behind the *bunker* the ball may
be dropped.

(iii) On the Putting Green: If the ball lies on the *putting
green*, the player must lift the ball and place it, without
penalty, at the *nearest point of relief* that is not in a *hazard*. The *nearest point of relief* may be off the *putting green*.

(iv) On the Teeing Ground: If the ball lies on the *teeing
ground*, the player must lift the ball and drop it, without
penalty, in accordance with Clause (i) above.

The ball may be cleaned when lifted under this Rule.

(Ball rolling to a position where there is interference by the
condition from which relief was taken — see Rule 20-2c(v).)

Exception: A player may not take relief under this Rule if
(a) it is clearly unreasonable for him to make a *stroke* because
of interference by anything other than an immovable *obstruction* or (b) interference by an immovable *obstruction* would
occur only through use of an unnecessarily abnormal *stance*,
swing or direction of play.

Note 1: If a ball is in a *water hazard* (including a *lateral water
hazard*), the player may not take relief from interference by an
immovable *obstruction*. The player must play the ball as it lies
or proceed under Rule 26-1.

Note 2: If a ball to be dropped or placed under this Rule is not
immediately recoverable, another ball may be *substituted*.

Note 3: The *Committee* may make a Local Rule stating that the
player must determine the *nearest point of relief* without crossing over, through or under the *obstruction*.

24-3. Ball in Obstruction Not Found

It is a question of fact whether a ball that has not been found after having been struck toward an *obstruction* is in the *obstruction*. In order to apply this Rule, it must be known or virtually certain that the ball is in the *obstruction*. In the absence of such knowledge or certainty, the player must proceed under Rule 27-1.

a. Ball in Movable Obstruction Not Found

If it is known or virtually certain that a ball that has not been found is in a movable *obstruction*, the player may *substitute* another ball and take relief without penalty under this Rule. If he elects to do so, he must remove the *obstruction* and *through the green* or in a *hazard* drop a ball, or on the *putting green* place a ball, as near as possible to the spot directly under the place where the ball last crossed the outermost limits of the movable *obstruction,* but not nearer the hole.

b. Ball in Immovable Obstruction Not Found

If it is known or virtually certain that a ball that has not been found is in an immovable *obstruction*, the player may take relief under this Rule. If he elects to do so, the spot where the ball last crossed the outermost limits of the *obstruction* must be determined and, for the purpose of applying this Rule, the ball is deemed to lie at this spot and the player must proceed as follows:

(i) Through the Green: If the ball last crossed the outermost limits of the immovable *obstruction* at a spot *through the green*, the player may *substitute* another ball, without penalty, and take relief as prescribed in Rule 24-2b(i).

(ii) In a Bunker: If the ball last crossed the outermost limits of the immovable *obstruction* at a spot in a *bunker*, the player may *substitute* another ball, without penalty, and take relief as prescribed in Rule 24-2b(ii).

(iii) In a Water Hazard (including a Lateral Water Hazard): If the ball last crossed the outermost limits of the immovable *obstruction* at a spot in a *water hazard,* the player is not entitled to relief without penalty. The player must proceed under Rule 26-1.

(iv) *On the Putting Green:* If the ball last crossed the outermost limits of the immovable *obstruction* at a spot on the *putting green*, the player may *substitute* another ball, without penalty, and take relief as prescribed in Rule 24-2b(iii).

PENALTY FOR BREACH OF RULE:
<u>Match play</u> — Loss of hole; <u>Stroke play</u> — Two strokes.

Rule 25. Abnormal Ground Conditions, Embedded Ball and Wrong Putting Green

Definitions
All defined terms are in *italics* and are listed alphabetically in the Definitions section — see pages 5–18.

25-1. Abnormal Ground Conditions

a. Interference
Interference by an *abnormal ground condition* occurs when a ball lies in or touches the condition or when the condition interferes with the player's *stance* or the area of his intended swing. If the player's ball lies on the *putting green*, interference also occurs if an *abnormal ground condition* on the *putting green* intervenes on his *line of putt*. Otherwise, intervention on the *line of play* is not, of itself, interference under this Rule.

Note: The *Committee* may make a Local Rule stating that interference by an *abnormal ground condition* with a player's *stance* is deemed not to be, of itself, interference under this Rule.

b. Relief
Except when the ball is in a *water hazard* or a *lateral water hazard*, a player may take relief from interference by an *abnormal ground condition* as follows:

(i) *Through the Green:* If the ball lies *through the green*, the player must lift the ball and drop it, without penalty, within one club-length of and not nearer the *hole* than the *nearest point of relief*. The *nearest point of relief* must not be in a *hazard* or on a *putting green*. When the ball is dropped within one club-length of the *nearest point of relief*, the ball must first strike a part of the *course* at a spot that avoids interference by the condition and is not in a *hazard* and not on a *putting green*.

(ii) In a Bunker: If the ball is in a *bunker*, the player must lift the ball and drop it either:

    (a) Without penalty, in accordance with Clause (i) above, except that the *nearest point of relief* must be in the *bunker* and the ball must be dropped in the *bunker* or, if complete relief is impossible, as near as possible to the spot where the ball lay, but not nearer the *hole*, on a part of the *course* in the *bunker* that affords maximum available relief from the condition; or

    (b) Under penalty of one stroke, outside the *bunker*, keeping the point where the ball lay directly between the *hole* and the spot on which the ball is dropped, with no limit to how far behind the *bunker* the ball may be dropped.

(iii) On the Putting Green: If the ball lies on the *putting green*, the player must lift the ball and place it, without penalty, at the *nearest point of relief* that is not in a *hazard* or, if complete relief is impossible, at the nearest position to where it lay that affords maximum available relief from the condition, but not nearer the *hole* and not in a *hazard*. The *nearest point of relief* or maximum available relief may be off the *putting green*.

(iv) On the Teeing Ground: If the ball lies on the *teeing ground*, the player must lift the ball and drop it, without penalty, in accordance with Clause (i) above.

The ball may be cleaned when lifted under Rule 25-1b.

(Ball rolling to a position where there is interference by the condition from which relief was taken — see Rule 20-2c(v).)

Exception: A player may not take relief under this Rule if

(a) it is clearly unreasonable for him to make a *stroke* because of interference by anything other than an *abnormal ground condition* or (b) interference by an *abnormal ground condition* would occur only through use of an unnecessarily abnormal *stance*, swing or direction of play.

Note 1: If a ball is in a *water hazard* (including a *lateral water hazard*), the player is not entitled to relief without penalty from interference by an *abnormal ground condition*. The player must play the ball as it lies (unless prohibited by Local Rule) or proceed under Rule 26-1.

Note 2: If a ball to be dropped or placed under this Rule is not immediately recoverable, another ball may be *substituted*.

c. Ball in Abnormal Ground Condition Not Found

It is a question of fact whether a ball that has not been found after having been struck toward an *abnormal ground condition* is in such a condition. In order to apply this Rule, it must be known or virtually certain that the ball is in the *abnormal ground condition*. In the absence of such knowledge or certainty, the player must proceed under Rule 27-1.

If it is known or virtually certain that a ball that has not been found is in an *abnormal ground condition*, the player may take relief under this Rule. If he elects to do so, the spot where the ball last crossed the outermost limits of the *abnormal ground condition* must be determined and, for the purpose of applying this Rule, the ball is deemed to lie at this spot and the player must proceed as follows:

(i) Through the Green: If the ball last crossed the outermost limits of the *abnormal ground condition* at a spot *through the green*, the player may *substitute* another ball, without penalty, and take relief as prescribed in Rule 25-1b(i).

(ii) In a Bunker: If the ball last crossed the outermost limits of the *abnormal ground condition* at a spot in a *bunker*, the player may *substitute* another ball, without penalty, and take relief as prescribed in Rule 25-1b(ii).

(iii) In a Water Hazard (including a Lateral Water Hazard): If the ball last crossed the outermost limits of the *abnormal ground condition* at a spot in a *water hazard*, the player is not entitled to relief without penalty. The player must proceed under Rule 26-1.

(iv) On the Putting Green: If the ball last crossed the outermost limits of the *abnormal ground condition* at a spot on the *putting green*, the player may *substitute* another ball, without penalty, and take relief as prescribed in Rule 25-1b(iii).

25-2. Embedded Ball

A ball embedded in its own pitch-mark in the ground in any closely mown area *through the green* may be lifted, cleaned and dropped, without penalty, as near as possible to the spot where it lay but not nearer the *hole*. The ball when dropped must first strike a part of the *course through the green*. "Closely mown area" means any area of the *course,* including paths through the rough, cut to fairway height or less.

25-3. Wrong Putting Green

a. Interference

Interference by a *wrong putting green* occurs when a ball is on the *wrong putting green*.

Interference to a player's *stance* or the area of his intended swing is not, of itself, interference under this Rule.

b. Relief

If a player's ball lies on a *wrong putting green*, he must not play the ball as it lies. He must take relief, without penalty, as follows:

The player must lift the ball and drop it within one club-length of and not nearer the *hole* than the *nearest point of relief*. The *nearest point of relief* must not be in a *hazard* or on a *putting green*. When dropping the ball within one club-length of the *nearest point of relief,* the ball must first strike a part of the *course* at a spot that avoids interference by the *wrong putting green* and is not in a *hazard* and not on a *putting green*. The ball may be cleaned when lifted under this Rule.

PENALTY FOR BREACH OF RULE:
<u>Match play</u> — Loss of hole; <u>Stroke play</u> — Two strokes.

Rule 26. Water Hazards
(Including Lateral Water Hazards)

Definitions

All defined terms are in *italics* and are listed alphabetically in the Definitions section — see pages 5-18.

26-1. Relief for Ball in Water Hazard

It is a question of fact whether a ball that has not been found after having been struck toward a *water hazard* is in the *hazard*. In order to apply this Rule, it must be known or virtually certain that the ball is in the *hazard*. In the absence of such knowledge or certainty, the player must proceed under Rule 27-1.

If a ball is in a *water hazard* or if it is known or virtually certain that a ball that has not been found is in a *water hazard* (whether the ball lies in water or not), the player may under penalty of one stroke:

    a. Play a ball as nearly as possible at the spot from which the original ball was last played (see Rule 20-5); or

    b. Drop a ball behind the *water hazard*, keeping the point at which the original ball last crossed the margin of the *water hazard* directly between the *hole* and the spot on which the ball is dropped, with no limit to how far behind the *water hazard* the ball may be dropped; or

    c. As additional options available only if the ball last crossed the margin of a *lateral water hazard*, drop a ball outside the *water hazard* within two club-lengths of and not nearer the *hole* than (i) the point where the original ball last crossed the margin of the *water hazard* or (ii) a point on the opposite margin of the *water hazard* equidistant from the *hole*.

When proceeding under this Rule, the player may lift and clean his ball or *substitute* a ball.

(Prohibited actions when ball is in hazard — see Rule 13-4.)

(Ball moving in water in a water hazard — see Rule 14-6.)

26-2. Ball Played Within Water Hazard

a. Ball Comes to Rest in Same or Another Water Hazard

If a ball played from within a *water hazard* comes to rest in the same or another *water hazard* after the *stroke*, the player may:

 (i) proceed under Rule 26-1a. If, after dropping in the *hazard,* the player elects not to play the dropped ball, he may:

  (a) proceed under Rule 26-1b, or if applicable Rule 26-1c, adding the additional penalty of one stroke prescribed by the Rule and using as the reference point the point where the original ball last crossed the margin of this *hazard* before it came to rest in this *hazard*; or

  (b) add an additional penalty of one stroke and play a ball as nearly as possible at the spot from which the last *stroke* from outside a *water hazard* was made (see Rule 20-5); or

 (ii) proceed under Rule 26-1b, or if applicable Rule 26-1c; or

 (iii) under penalty of one stroke, play a ball as nearly as possible at the spot from which the last *stroke* from outside a *water hazard* was made (see Rule 20-5).

b. Ball Lost or Unplayable Outside Hazard or Out of Bounds

If a ball played from within a *water hazard* is *lost* or deemed unplayable outside the *hazard* or is *out of bounds*, the player may, after taking a penalty of one stroke under Rule 27-1 or 28a:

 (i) play a ball as nearly as possible at the spot in the *hazard* from which the original ball was last played (see Rule 20-5); or

 (ii) proceed under Rule 26-1b, or if applicable Rule 26-1c, adding the additional penalty of one stroke prescribed by the Rule and using as the reference point the point where the original ball last crossed the margin of the *hazard* before it came to rest in the *hazard*; or

 (iii) add an additional penalty of one stroke and play a ball as nearly as possible at the spot from which the last *stroke* from outside a *water hazard* was made (see Rule 20-5).

Note 1: When proceeding under Rule 26-2b, the player is not required to drop a ball under Rule 27-1 or 28a. If he does drop a ball, he is not required to play it. He may alternatively proceed under Rule 26-2b(ii) or (iii).

Note 2: If a ball played from within a *water hazard* is deemed unplayable outside the *hazard*, nothing in Rule 26-2b precludes the player from proceeding under Rule 28b or c.

PENALTY FOR BREACH OF RULE:
Match play — Loss of hole; Stroke play — Two strokes.

Rule 27.
Ball Lost or Out of Bounds; Provisional Ball

Definitions
All defined terms are in *italics* and are listed alphabetically in the Definitions section — see pages 5-18.

27-1. Stroke and Distance; Ball Out of Bounds; Ball Not Found Within Five Minutes

a. Proceeding Under Stroke and Distance
At any time, a player may, under penalty of one stroke, play a ball as nearly as possible at the spot from which the original ball was last played (see Rule 20-5), i.e., proceed under penalty of stroke and distance.

Except as otherwise provided in the *Rules*, if a player makes a *stroke* at a ball from the spot at which the original ball was last played, he is deemed to have proceeded under penalty of stroke and distance.

b. Ball Out of Bounds
If a ball is *out of bounds*, the player must play a ball, under penalty of one stroke, as nearly as possible at the spot from which the original ball was last played (see Rule 20-5).

c. Ball Not Found Within Five Minutes

If a ball is *lost* as a result of not being found or identified as his by the player within five minutes after the player's *side* or his or their *caddies* have begun to search for it, the player must play a ball, under penalty of one stroke, as nearly as possible at the spot from which the original ball was last played (see Rule 20-5).

Exceptions:

1. If it is known or virtually certain that the original ball that has not been found is in an *obstruction* (Rule 24-3) or is in an *abnormal ground condition* (Rule 25-1c), the player may proceed under the applicable *Rule*.

2. If it is known or virtually certain that the original ball that has not been found has been moved by an *outside agency* (Rule 18-1) or is in a *water hazard* (Rule 26-1), the player must proceed under the applicable *Rule*.

PENALTY FOR BREACH OF RULE 27-1:

<u>Match play</u> — Loss of hole; <u>Stroke play</u> — Two strokes.

27-2. Provisional Ball

a. Procedure

If a ball may be *lost* outside a *water hazard* or may be *out of bounds*, to save time the player may play another ball provisionally in accordance with Rule 27-1. The player must inform his opponent in match play or his *marker* or a *fellow-competitor* in stroke play that he intends to play a *provisional ball*, and he must play it before he or his *partner* goes forward to search for the original ball.

If he fails to do so and plays another ball, that ball is not a *provisional ball* and becomes the *ball in play* under penalty of stroke and distance (Rule 27-1); the original ball is *lost*.

Order of play from teeing ground — see Rule 10-3.)

Note: If a *provisional ball* played under Rule 27-2a might be lost outside a *water hazard* or *out of bounds,* the player may play another *provisional ball*. If another *provisional ball* is played, it bears the same relationship to the previous *provisional ball* as the first *provisional ball* bears to the original ball.

b. When Provisional Ball Becomes Ball in Play

The player may play a *provisional ball* until he reaches the place where the original ball is likely to be. If he makes a *stroke* with the *provisional ball* from the place where the original ball is likely to be or from a point nearer the *hole* than that place, the original ball is *lost* and the *provisional ball* becomes the *ball in play* under penalty of stroke and distance (**Rule 27-1**).

If the original ball is *lost* outside a *water hazard* or is *out of bounds*, the *provisional ball* becomes the *ball in play*, under penalty of stroke and distance (Rule 27-1).

If it is known or virtually certain that the original ball is in a *water hazard*, the player must proceed in accordance with Rule 26-1.

Exception: If it is known or virtually certain that the original ball is in an *obstruction* (Rule 24-3) or an *abnormal ground condition* (Rule 25-1c), the player may proceed under the applicable *Rule*.

c. When Provisional Ball to Be Abandoned

If the original ball is neither *lost* nor *out of bounds*, the player must abandon the *provisional ball* and continue playing the original ball. If he makes any further *strokes* at the *provisional ball*, he is playing a *wrong ball* and the provisions of Rule 15-3 apply.

Note: If a player plays a *provisional ball* under Rule 27-2a, the *strokes* made after this Rule has been invoked with a *provisional ball* subsequently abandoned under Rule 27-2c and *penalty strokes* incurred solely by playing that ball are disregarded.

Rule 28. Ball Unplayable

Definitions

All defined terms are in *italics* and are listed alphabetically in the Definitions section — see pages 5-18.

The player may deem his ball unplayable at any place on the *course*, except when the ball is in a *water hazard*. The player is the sole judge as to whether his ball is unplayable.

If the player deems his ball to be unplayable, he must, under penalty of one stroke:

a. Play a ball as nearly as possible at the spot from which the original ball was last played (see Rule 20-5); or

b. Drop a ball behind the point where the ball lay, keeping that point directly between the *hole* and the spot on which the ball is dropped, with no limit to how far behind that point the ball may be dropped; or

c. Drop a ball within two club-lengths of the spot where the ball lay, but not nearer the *hole*.

If the unplayable ball is in a *bunker*, the player may proceed under Clause a, b or c. If he elects to proceed under Clause b or c, a ball must be dropped in the *bunker*.

When proceeding under this Rule, the player may lift and clean his ball or *substitute* a ball.

PENALTY FOR BREACH OF RULE:

<u>Match play</u> — Loss of hole; <u>Stroke play</u> — Two strokes.

OTHER FORMS OF PLAY

Rule 29. Threesomes and Foursomes

Definitions

All defined terms are in *italics* and are listed alphabetically in the Definitions section — see pages 5-18.

29-1. General

In a *threesome* or a *foursome*, during any *stipulated round* the *partners* must play alternately from the *teeing grounds* and alternately during the play of each hole. *Penalty strokes* do not affect the order of play.

29-2. Match Play

If a player plays when his *partner* should have played, his *side* loses the hole.

29-3. Stroke Play

If the *partners* make a *stroke* or *strokes* in incorrect order, such *stroke* or *strokes* are canceled and the *side* incurs a penalty of two strokes. The *side* must correct the error by playing a ball in correct order as nearly as possible at the spot from which it first played in incorrect order (see Rule 20-5). If the *side* makes a *stroke* on the next *teeing ground* without first correcting the error or, in the case of the last hole of the round, leaves the *putting green* without declaring its intention to correct the error, the *side* is disqualified.

Rule 30. Three-Ball, Best-Ball and Four-Ball Match Play

Definitions

All defined terms are in *italics* and are listed alphabetically in the Definitions section — see pages 5-18.

30-1. Rules of Golf Apply

The Rules of Golf, so far as they are not at variance with the ollowing specific Rules, apply to *three-ball, best-ball* and *four-ball* natches.

30-2. Three-Ball Match Play

a. Ball at Rest Moved by an Opponent

Except as otherwise provided in the *Rules*, if the player's ball is touched or *moved* by an opponent, his *caddie* or *equipment* other han during search, Rule 18-3b applies. That opponent incurs a penalty of one stroke in his match with the player, but not n his match with the other opponent.

b. Ball Deflected or Stopped by an Opponent Accidentally

f a player's ball is accidentally deflected or stopped by an opponent, his *caddie* or *equipment*, there is no penalty. In his match with that opponent the player may, before another *stroke* is made by either *side*, cancel the *stroke* and play a ball, without penalty, as nearly as possible at the spot from which the original ball was last played (see Rule 20-5) or he may play the ball as it lies. In his match with the other opponent, the ball must be played as it lies.

Exception: Ball striking person attending or holding up *flagstick* or anything carried by him — see Rule 17-3b.

Ball purposely deflected or stopped by opponent — see Rule 1-2.)

30-3. Best-Ball and Four-Ball Match Play

a. Representation of Side

A *side* may be represented by one *partner* for all or any part of a match; all *partners* need not be present. An absent *partner* may join a match between holes, but not during play of a hole.

b. Order of Play

Balls belonging to the same *side* may be played in the order the *side* considers best.

c. Wrong Ball

f a player incurs the loss of hole penalty under Rule 15-3a for making a *stroke* at a *wrong ball*, he is disqualified for that hole, but his *partner* incurs no penalty even if the *wrong ball* belongs to him. If the *wrong ball* belongs to another player, its owner must place a ball on the spot from which the *wrong ball* was first played.

d. Penalty to Side

A *side* is penalized for a breach of any of the following by any *partner*:

- Rule 4 — Clubs
- Rule 6-4 — Caddie
- Any Local Rule or Condition of Competition for which the penalty is an adjustment to the state of the match.

e. Disqualification of Side

(i) A *side* is disqualified if any *partner* incurs a penalty of disqualification under any of the following:

- Rule 1-3 — Agreement to Waive Rules
- Rule 4 — Clubs
- Rule 5-1 or 5-2 — The Ball
- Rule 6-2a — Handicap
- Rule 6-4 — Caddie
- Rule 6-7 — Undue Delay; Slow Play
- Rule 11-1 — Teeing
- Rule 14-3 — Artificial Devices, Unusual Equipment and Unusual Use of Equipment
- Rule 33-7 — Disqualification Penalty Imposed by Committee

(ii) A *side* is disqualified if all *partners* incur a penalty of disqualification under any of the following:

- Rule 6-3 — Time of Starting and Groups
- Rule 6-8 — Discontinuance of Play

(iii) In all other cases where a breach of a *Rule* would result in disqualification, the player is disqualified for that hole only.

f. Effect of Other Penalties

If a player's breach of a *Rule* assists his *partner's* play or adversely

ffects an opponent's play, the *partner* incurs the applicable pen-
lty in addition to any penalty incurred by the player.

n all other cases where a player incurs a penalty for breach
f a *Rule*, the penalty does not apply to his *partner*. Where the
enalty is stated to be loss of hole, the effect is to disqualify
he player for that hole.

Rule 31. Four-Ball Stroke Play

Definitions

ll defined terms are in *italics* and are listed alphabetically in
he Definitions section — see pages 5-18.

31-1. General

he Rules of Golf, so far as they are not at variance with the fol-
owing specific Rules, apply to *four-ball* stroke play.

31-2. Representation of Side

side may be represented by either *partner* for all or any part of
stipulated round; both *partners* need not be present. An absent
ompetitor may join his *partner* between holes, but not during
lay of a hole.

31-3. Scoring

he *marker* is required to record for each hole only the gross
core of whichever *partner's* score is to count. The gross scores
o count must be individually identifiable; otherwise, the *side*
disqualified. Only one of the *partners* need be responsible for
omplying with Rule 6-6b.

Wrong score — see Rule 31-7a.)

31-4. Order of Play

alls belonging to the same *side* may be played in the order the
de considers best.

31-5. Wrong Ball

a *competitor* is in breach of Rule 15-3b for making a *stroke* at a
rong ball*, he incurs a penalty of two strokes and must correct

his mistake by playing the correct ball or by proceeding under the *Rules*. His *partner* incurs no penalty even if the *wrong ball* belongs to him.

If the *wrong ball* belongs to another *competitor*, its owner must place a ball on the spot from which the *wrong ball* was first played.

31-6. Penalty to Side

A *side* is penalized for a breach of any of the following by either *partner*:

- Rule 4 — Clubs
- Rule 6-4 — Caddie
- Any Local Rule or Condition of Competition for which there is a maximum penalty per round.

31-7. Disqualification Penalties

a. Breach by One Partner

A *side* is disqualified from the competition if either *partner* incurs a penalty of disqualification under any of the following

- Rule 1-3 — Agreement to Waive Rules
- Rule 3-4 — Refusal to Comply with a Rule
- Rule 4 — Clubs
- Rule 5-1 or 5-2 — The Ball
- Rule 6-2b — Handicap
- Rule 6-4 — Caddie
- Rule 6-6b — Signing and Returning Score Card
- Rule 6-6d — Wrong Score for Hole
- Rule 6-7 — Undue Delay; Slow Play
- Rule 7-1 — Practice Before or Between Rounds
- Rule 11-1 — Teeing
- Rule 14-3 — Artificial Devices, Unusual Equipment and Unusual Use of Equipment

- Rule 22-1 — Ball Assisting Play
- Rule 31-3 — Gross Scores to Count Not Individually Identifiable
- Rule 33-7 — Disqualification Penalty Imposed by Committee

b. Breach by Both Partners

A *side* is disqualified from the competition:

(i) if each *partner* incurs a penalty of disqualification for a breach of Rule 6-3 (Time of Starting and Groups) or Rule 6-8 (Discontinuance of Play), or

(ii) if, at the same hole, each *partner* is in breach of a *Rule* the penalty for which is disqualification from the competition or for a hole.

c. For the Hole Only

In all other cases where a breach of a *Rule* would result in disqualification, the *competitor* is disqualified only for the hole at which the breach occurred.

31-8. Effect of Other Penalties

If a *competitor's* breach of a *Rule* assists his *partner's* play, the *partner* incurs the applicable penalty in addition to any penalty incurred by the *competitor*.

In all other cases where a *competitor* incurs a penalty for breach of a *Rule*, the penalty does not apply to his *partner*.

Rule 32.
Bogey, Par and Stableford Competitions

Definitions
All defined terms are in *italics* and are listed alphabetically in the Definitions section — see pages 5-18.

32-1. Conditions

Bogey, par and Stableford competitions are forms of stroke play in which play is against a fixed score at each hole. The *Rules* for stroke play, so far as they are not at variance with the following specific Rules, apply.

In handicap bogey, par and Stableford competitions, the *competitor* with the lowest net score at a hole takes the *honor* at the next *teeing ground*.

a. Bogey and Par Competitions
The scoring for bogey and par competitions is made as in match play. Any hole for which a *competitor* makes no return is regarded as a loss. The winner is the *competitor* who is most successful in the aggregate of holes.

The *marker* is responsible for marking only the gross number of *strokes* for each hole where the *competitor* makes a net score equal to or less than the fixed score.

Note 1: The *competitor's* score is adjusted by deducting a hole or holes under the applicable *Rule* when a penalty other than disqualification is incurred under any of the following:

- Rule 4 — Clubs
- Rule 6-4 — Caddie
- Any Local Rule or Condition of Competition for which there is a maximum penalty per round.

The *competitor* is responsible for reporting the facts regarding such a breach to the *Committee* before he returns his score card so that the *Committee* may apply the penalty. If the *competitor* fails to report his breach to the *Committee*, he is disqualified.

Note 2: If the *competitor* is in breach of Rule 6-7 (Undue Delay; Slow Play), the *Committee* will deduct one hole from the aggregate of holes. For a repeated offense, see Rule 32-2a.

b. Stableford Competitions

The scoring in Stableford competitions is made by points awarded in relation to a fixed score at each hole as follows:

Hole Played In	Points
More than one over fixed score or no score returned	0
One over fixed score	1
Fixed score	2
One under fixed score	3
Two under fixed score	4
Three under fixed score	5
Four under fixed score	6

The winner is the *competitor* who scores the highest number of points.

The *marker* is responsible for marking only the gross number of strokes at each hole where the *competitor's* net score earns one or more points.

Note 1: If a *competitor* is in breach of a *Rule* for which there is a maximum penalty per round, he must report the facts to the *Committee* before returning his score card; if he fails to do so, he is disqualified. The *Committee* will, from the total points scored for the round, deduct two points for each hole at which any breach occurred, with a maximum deduction per round of four points for each Rule breached.

Note 2: If the *competitor* is in breach of Rule 6-7 (Undue Delay; Slow Play), the *Committee* will deduct two points from the total points scored for the round. For a repeated offense, see Rule 32-2a.

32-2. Disqualification Penalties

a. From the Competition

A *competitor* is disqualified from the competition if he incurs a penalty of disqualification under any of the following:

- Rule 1-3 — Agreement to Waive Rules
- Rule 3-4 — Refusal to Comply with Rule
- Rule 4 — Clubs
- Rule 5-1 or 5-2 — The Ball
- Rule 6-2b — Handicap
- Rule 6-3 — Time of Starting and Groups
- Rule 6-4 — Caddie
- Rule 6-6b — Signing and Returning Score Card
- Rule 6-6d — Wrong Score for Hole, i.e., when the recorded score is lower than actually taken, except that no penalty is incurred when a breach of this Rule does not affect the result of the hole
- Rule 6-7 — Undue Delay; Slow Play
- Rule 6-8 — Discontinuance of Play
- Rule 7-1 — Practice Before or Between Rounds
- Rule 11-1 — Teeing
- Rule 14-3 — Artificial Devices, Unusual Equipment and Unusual Use of Equipment
- Rule 22-1 — Ball Assisting Play
- Rule 33-7 — Disqualification Penalty Imposed by Committee

b. For a Hole

In all other cases where a breach of a *Rule* would result in disqualification, the *competitor* is disqualified only for the hole at which the breach occurred.

ADMINISTRATION

Rule 33. The Committee

Definitions

All defined terms are in *italics* and are listed alphabetically in the Definitions section — see pages 5-18.

33-1. Conditions; Waiving Rule

The *Committee* must establish the conditions under which a competition is to be played.

The *Committee* has no power to waive a Rule of Golf.

Certain specific *Rules* governing stroke play are so substantially different from those governing match play that combining the two forms of play is not practicable and is not permitted. The result of a match played in these circumstances is null and void and, in the stroke-play competition, the *competitors* are disqualified.

In stroke play, the *Committee* may limit a *referee's* duties.

33-2. The Course

a. Defining Bounds and Margins

The *Committee* must define accurately:

   (i) the *course* and *out of bounds*,

  (ii) the margins of *water hazards* and *lateral water hazards*,

 (iii) *ground under repair*, and

 (iv) *obstructions* and integral parts of the *course*.

b. New Holes

New *holes* should be made on the day on which a stroke-play competition begins and at such other times as the *Committee* considers necessary, provided all *competitors* in a single round play with each *hole* cut in the same position.

Exception: When it is impossible for a damaged *hole* to be repaired so that it conforms with the Definition, the *Committee* may make a new *hole* in a nearby similar position.

Note: Where a single round is to be played on more than one day, the *Committee* may provide, in the conditions of a competition (Rule 33-1), that the *holes* and *teeing grounds* may be differently situated on each day of the competition, provided that, on any one day, all *competitors* play with each *hole* and each *teeing ground* in the same position.

c. Practice Ground

Where there is no practice ground available outside the area of a competition *course*, the *Committee* should establish the area on which players may practice on any day of a competition, if it is practicable to do so. On any day of a stroke-play competition, the *Committee* should not normally permit practice on or to a *putting green* or from a *hazard* of the competition *course*.

d. Course Unplayable

If the *Committee* or its authorized representative considers that for any reason the *course* is not in a playable condition or that there are circumstances that render the proper playing of the game impossible, it may, in match play or stroke play, order a temporary suspension of play or, in stroke play, declare play null and void and cancel all scores for the round in question. When a round is canceled, all penalties incurred in that round are canceled.

(Procedure in discontinuing and resuming play — see Rule 6-8.)

33-3. Times of Starting and Groups

The *Committee* must establish the times of starting and, in stroke play, arrange the groups in which *competitors* must play.

When a match-play competition is played over an extended period, the *Committee* establishes the limit of time within which each round must be completed. When players are allowed to arrange the date of their match within these limits, the *Committee* should announce that the match must be played at a stated time on the last day of the period, unless the players agree to a prior date.

33-4. Handicap Stroke Table

The *Committee* must publish a table indicating the order of holes at which handicap strokes are to be given or received.

33-5. Score Card

In stroke play, the *Committee* must provide each *competitor* with a score card containing the date and the *competitor's* name or, in *foursomes* or *four-ball* stroke play, the *competitors'* names.

In stroke play, the *Committee* is responsible for the addition of scores and the application of the handicap recorded on the score card.

In *four-ball* stroke play, the *Committee* is responsible for recording the better-ball score for each hole and in the process applying the handicaps recorded on the score card, and adding the better-ball scores.

In bogey, par and Stableford competitions, the *Committee* is responsible for applying the handicap recorded on the score card and determining the result of each hole and the overall result or points total.

Note: The *Committee* may request that each *competitor* record the date and his name on his score card.

33-6. Decision of Ties

The *Committee* must announce the manner, day and time for the decision of a halved match or of a tie, whether played on level terms or under handicap.

A halved match must not be decided by stroke play. A tie in stroke play must not be decided by a match.

33-7. Disqualification Penalty; Committee Discretion

A penalty of disqualification may in exceptional individual cases be waived, modified or imposed if the *Committee* considers such action warranted.

Any penalty less than disqualification must not be waived or modified.

If a *Committee* considers that a player is guilty of a serious breach of etiquette, it may impose a penalty of disqualification under this Rule.

33-8. Local Rules

a. Policy

The *Committee* may establish Local Rules for local abnormal conditions if they are consistent with the policy set forth in Appendix I.

b. Waiving or Modifying a Rule

A Rule of Golf must not be waived by a Local Rule. However, if a *Committee* considers that local abnormal conditions interfere with the proper playing of the game to the extent that it is necessary to make a Local Rule that modifies the Rules of Golf, the Local Rule must be authorized by the USGA.

Rule 34. Disputes and Decisions

Definitions

All defined terms are in *italics* and are listed alphabetically in the Definitions section — see pages 5-18.

34-1. Claims and Penalties

a. Match Play

If a claim is lodged with the *Committee* under Rule 2-5, a decision should be given as soon as possible so that the state of the match may, if necessary, be adjusted. If a claim is not made in accordance with Rule 2-5, it must not be considered by the *Committee*.

There is no time limit on applying the disqualification penalty for a breach of Rule 1-3.

b. Stroke Play

In stroke play, a penalty must not be rescinded, modified or imposed after the competition has closed. A competition is closed when the result has been officially announced or, in stroke-play qualifying followed by match play, when the player has teed off in his first match.

Exceptions: A penalty of disqualification must be imposed after the competition has closed if a *competitor*:

(i) was in breach of Rule 1-3 (Agreement to Waive Rules); or

(ii) returned a score card on which he had recorded a handicap that, before the competition closed, he knew was higher than that to which he was entitled, and this affected the number of strokes received (Rule 6-2b); or

(iii) returned a score for any hole lower than actually taken (Rule 6-6d) for any reason other than failure to include a penalty that, before the competition closed, he did not know he had incurred; or

(iv) knew, before the competition closed, that he had been in breach of any other *Rule* for which the penalty is disqualification.

34-2. Referee's Decision

If a *referee* has been appointed by the *Committee*, his decision is final.

34-3. Committee's Decision

In the absence of a *referee*, any dispute or doubtful point on the *Rules* must be referred to the *Committee*, whose decision is final.

If the *Committee* cannot come to a decision, it may refer the dispute or doubtful point to the Rules of Golf Committee of the United States Golf Association, whose decision is final.

If the dispute or doubtful point has not been referred to the Rules of Golf Committee, the player or players may request that an agreed statement be referred through a duly authorized representative of the *Committee* to the Rules of Golf Committee for an opinion as to the correctness of the decision given. The reply will be sent to this authorized representative.

If play is conducted other than in accordance with the Rules of Golf, the Rules of Golf Committee will not give a decision on any question.

APPENDIX I

CONTENTS

APPENDIX I LOCAL RULES; CONDITIONS OF THE COMPETITION

Definitions

All defined terms are in *italics* and are listed alphabetically in the Definitions section — see pages 5-18.

PART A: *LOCAL RULES*

As provided in Rule 33-8a, the *Committee* may make and publish Local Rules for local abnormal conditions if they are consistent with the policy established in this Appendix. In addition, detailed information regarding acceptable and prohibited Local Rules is provided in "Decisions on the Rules of Golf" under Rule 33-8 and in "How to Conduct a Competition."

If local abnormal conditions interfere with the proper playing of the game and the *Committee* considers it necessary to modify a Rule of Golf, authorization from the United States Golf Association must be obtained.

1. Defining Bounds and Margins

Specifying means used to define *out of bounds*, *water hazards*, *lateral water hazards*, *ground under repair*, *obstructions* and integral parts of the *course* (Rule 33-2a).

2. Water Hazards

a. Lateral Water Hazards

Clarifying the status of *water hazards* that may be *lateral water hazards* (Rule 26).

b. Ball Played Provisionally Under Rule 26-1

Permitting play of a ball provisionally under Rule 26-1 for a ball that may be in a *water hazard* (including a *lateral water hazard*) of such character that, if the original ball is not found, it is known or virtually certain that it is in the *water hazard* and it would be impracticable to determine whether the ball is in the *hazard* or to do so would unduly delay play.

3. Areas of the Course Requiring Preservation; Environmentally-Sensitive Areas

Assisting preservation of the *course* by defining areas, including turf nurseries, young plantations and other parts of the *course* under cultivation, as *ground under repair* from which play is prohibited.

When the *Committee* is required to prohibit play from environmentally-sensitive areas that are on or adjoin the *course*, it should make a Local Rule clarifying the relief procedure.

4. Course Conditions — Mud, Extreme Wetness, Poor Conditions and Protection of the Course

a. Lifting an Embedded Ball; Cleaning

Course conditions that might interfere with proper playing of the game, including mud and extreme wetness, warranting relief for an embedded ball anywhere *through the green* or permitting lifting, cleaning and replacing a ball anywhere *through the green* or on a closely mown area *through the green*.

b. "Preferred Lies" and "Winter Rules"

Adverse conditions, including the poor condition of the *course* or the existence of mud, are sometimes so general, particularly during winter months, that the *Committee* may decide to grant relief by temporary Local Rule either to protect the *course* or to promote fair and pleasant play. The Local Rule should be withdrawn as soon as the conditions warrant.

5. Obstructions

a. General

Clarifying the status of objects that may be *obstructions* (Rule 24).

Declaring any construction to be an integral part of the *course* and, accordingly, not an *obstruction*, e.g., built-up sides of *teeing grounds*, *putting greens* and *bunkers* (Rules 24 and 33-2a).

b. Stones in Bunkers

Allowing the removal of stones in *bunkers* by declaring them to be movable *obstructions* (Rule 24-1).

c. Roads and Paths
(i) Declaring artificial surfaces and sides of roads and paths to be integral parts of the *course*, or

(ii) Providing relief of the type afforded under Rule 24-2b from roads and paths not having artificial surfaces and sides, if they could unfairly affect play.

d. Immovable Obstructions Close to Putting Green
Providing relief from intervention by immovable *obstructions* on or within two club-lengths of the *putting green* when the ball lies within two club-lengths of the immovable *obstruction*.

e. Protection of Young Trees
Providing relief for the protection of young trees.

f. Temporary Obstructions
Providing relief from interference by temporary *obstructions* (e.g., grandstands, television cables and equipment, etc.).

6. Dropping Zones

Establishing special areas on which balls may or must be dropped when it is not feasible or practicable to proceed exactly in conformity with Rule 24-2b (Immovable Obstruction), Rule 24-3 (Ball in Obstruction Not Found), Rule 25-1b or 25-1c (Abnormal Ground Conditions), Rule 25-3 (Wrong Putting Green), Rule 26-1 (Water Hazards and Lateral Water Hazards) or Rule 28 (Ball Unplayable).

PART B: SPECIMEN LOCAL RULES

Within the policy established in Part A of this Appendix, the *Committee* may adopt a Specimen Local Rule by referring, on a score card or notice board, to the examples given below. However, Specimen Local Rules of a temporary nature should not be printed on a score card.

1. Water Hazards; Ball Played Provisionally Under Rule 26-1

If a *water hazard* (including a *lateral water hazard*) is of such size and shape and/or located in such a position that:

(i) it would be impracticable to determine whether the ball is in the *hazard* or to do so would unduly delay play, and

(ii) if the original ball is not found, it is known or virtually certain that it is in the *water hazard*,

the *Committee* may introduce a Local Rule permitting the play of a ball provisionally under Rule 26-1. The ball is played provisionally under any of the applicable options under Rule 26-1 or any applicable Local Rule. In such a case, if a ball is played provisionally and the original ball is in a *water hazard*, the player may play the original ball as it lies or continue with the ball played provisionally, but he may not proceed under Rule 26-1 with regard to the original ball.

In these circumstances, the following Local Rule is recommended:

"If there is doubt whether a ball is in or is *lost* in the *water hazard* (specify location), the player may play another ball provisionally under any of the applicable options in Rule 26-1.

If the original ball is found outside the *water hazard*, the player must continue play with it.

If the original ball is found in the *water hazard*, the player may either play the original ball as it lies or continue with the ball played provisionally under Rule 26-1.

If the original ball is not found or identified within the five-minute search period, the player must continue with the ball played provisionally.

PENALTY FOR BREACH OF LOCAL RULE:
Match play — Loss of hole; Stroke play — Two strokes."

2. Areas of the Course Requiring Preservation; Environmentally-Sensitive Areas

a. Ground Under Repair; Play Prohibited

If the *Committee* wishes to protect any area of the *course*, it should declare it to be *ground under repair* and prohibit play from within that area. The following Local Rule is recommended:

"The _____(defined by _____) is *ground under repair* from which play is prohibited. If a player's ball lies in the area, or if it interferes with the player's *stance* or the area of his intended swing, the player must take relief under Rule 25-1.

PENALTY FOR BREACH OF LOCAL RULE:
Match play — Loss of hole; Stroke play — Two strokes."

b. Environmentally-Sensitive Areas

If an appropriate authority (i.e., a government agency or the like) prohibits entry into and/or play from an area on or adjoining the *course* for environmental reasons, the *Committee* should make a Local Rule clarifying the relief procedure.

The *Committee* has some discretion in terms of whether the area is defined as *ground under repair*, a *water hazard* or *out of bounds*. However, it may not simply define such an area to be a *water hazard* if it does not meet the Definition of a "*Water Hazard*" and it should attempt to preserve the character of the hole.

The following Local Rule is recommended:

"**I. Definition**
An environmentally-sensitive area (ESA) is an area so declared by an appropriate authority, entry into and/or play from which is prohibited for environmental reasons. These areas may be defined as *ground under repair*, a *water hazard*, a *lateral water hazard* or *out of bounds* at the discretion of the *Committee*, provided that in the case of an ESA that has been defined as a *water hazard* or a *lateral water hazard*, the area is, by Definition, a *water hazard*.

Note: The *Committee* may not declare an area to be environmentally-sensitive.

II. Ball in Environmentally-Sensitive Area
a. Ground Under Repair
If a ball is in an ESA defined as *ground under repair*, a ball must be dropped in accordance with Rule 25-1b.

If it is known or virtually certain that a ball that has not been found is in an ESA defined as *ground under repair*, the player may take relief, without penalty, as prescribed in Rule 25-1c.

b. Water Hazards and Lateral Water Hazards

If it is known or virtually certain that a ball that has not been found is in an ESA defined as a *water hazard* or *lateral water hazard,* the player must, under penalty of one stroke, proceed under Rule 26-1.

Note: If a ball dropped in accordance with Rule 26 rolls into a position where the ESA interferes with the player's *stance* or the area of his intended swing, the player must take relief as provided in Clause III of this Local Rule.

c. Out of Bounds

If a ball is in an ESA defined as *out of bounds*, the player must play a ball, under penalty of one stroke, as nearly as possible at the spot from which the original ball was last played (see Rule 20-5).

III. Interference with Stance or Area of Intended Swing

Interference by an ESA occurs when the ESA interferes with the player's *stance* or the area of his intended swing. If interference exists, the player must take relief as follows:

(a) Through the Green: If the ball lies *through the green*, the point on the *course* nearest to where the ball lies must be determined that (a) is not nearer the *hole*, (b) avoids interference by the ESA and (c) is not in a *hazard* or on a *putting green*. The player must lift the ball and drop it, without penalty, within one club-length of the point so determined on a part of the *course* that fulfills (a), (b) and (c) above.

(b) In a Hazard: If the ball is in a *hazard*, the player must lift the ball and drop it either:

(i) Without penalty, in the *hazard*, as near as possible to the spot where the ball lay, but not nearer the *hole*, on a part of the *course* that provides complete relief from the ESA; or

(ii) Under penalty of one stroke, outside the *hazard*, keeping the point where the ball lay directly between the *hole* and the spot on which the ball is dropped, with no limit to how far behind the *hazard* the ball may be dropped. Additionally, the player may proceed under Rule 26 or 28 if applicable.

(c) On the Putting Green: If the ball lies on the *putting green*, the player must lift the ball and place it, without penalty, in the nearest position to where it lay that affords complete relief from the ESA, but not nearer the *hole* or in a *hazard*.

The ball may be cleaned when lifted under Clause III of this Local Rule.

Exception: A player may not take relief under Clause III of this Local Rule if (a) it is clearly unreasonable for him to make a *stroke* because of interference by anything other than an ESA or (b) interference by an ESA would occur only through use of an unnecessarily abnormal *stance*, swing or direction of play.

PENALTY FOR BREACH OF LOCAL RULE:
Match play — Loss of hole; Stroke play — Two strokes.

Note: In the case of a serious breach of this Local Rule, the *Committee* may impose a penalty of disqualification."

3. Protection of Young Trees

When it is desired to prevent damage to young trees, the following Local Rule is recommended:

"Protection of young trees identified by _____ — If such a tree interferes with a player's *stance* or the area of his intended swing, the ball must be lifted, without penalty, and dropped in accordance with the procedure prescribed in Rule 24-2b (Immovable Obstruction). If the ball lies in a *water hazard*, the player must lift and drop the ball in accordance with Rule 24-2b(i), except that the *nearest point of relief* must be in the *water hazard* and the ball must be dropped in the *water hazard*, or the player may proceed under Rule 26. The ball may be cleaned when lifted under this Local Rule.

Exception: A player may not take relief under this Local Rule if (a) it is clearly unreasonable for him to make a *stroke* because of interference by anything other than the tree or (b) interference by the tree would occur only through use of an unnecessarily abnormal *stance*, swing or direction of play.

PENALTY FOR BREACH OF LOCAL RULE:
Match play — Loss of hole; Stroke play — Two strokes."

4. Course Conditions — Mud, Extreme Wetness, Poor Conditions and Protection of the Course

a. Relief for Embedded Ball

Rule 25-2 provides relief, without penalty, for a ball embedded in its own pitch-mark in any closely mown area *through the green*. On the *putting green*, a ball may be lifted and damage caused by the impact of a ball may be repaired (Rules 16-1b and c). When permission to take relief for an embedded ball anywhere *through the green* would be warranted, the following Local Rule is recommended:

"*Through the green*, a ball that is embedded in its own pitch-mark in the ground may be lifted, without penalty, cleaned and dropped as near as possible to where it lay but not nearer the *hole*. The ball when dropped must first strike a part of the *course through the green*.

Exceptions:

1. A player may not take relief under this Local Rule if the ball is embedded in sand in an area that is not closely mown.

2. A player may not take relief under this Local Rule if it is clearly unreasonable for him to make a *stroke* because of interference by anything other than the condition covered by this Local Rule.

PENALTY FOR BREACH OF LOCAL RULE:
Match play — Loss of hole; Stroke play — Two strokes."

b. Cleaning Ball

Conditions, such as extreme wetness causing significant amounts of mud to adhere to the ball, may be such that permission to lift, clean and replace the ball would be appropriate. In these circumstances, the following Local Rule is recommended:

"(Specify area) a ball may be lifted, cleaned and replaced without penalty.

Note: The position of the ball must be marked before it is lifted under this Local Rule — see Rule 20-1.

PENALTY FOR BREACH OF LOCAL RULE:
Match play — Loss of hole; Stroke play — Two strokes."

c. "Preferred Lies" and "Winter Rules"

Ground under repair is provided for in Rule 25, and occasional local abnormal conditions that might interfere with fair play and are not widespread should be defined as *ground under repair*.

However, adverse conditions, such as heavy snows, spring thaws, prolonged rains or extreme heat can make fairways unsatisfactory and sometimes prevent use of heavy mowing equipment. When these conditions are so general throughout a *course* that the *Committee* believes "preferred lies" or "winter rules" would promote fair play or help protect the *course*, the following Local Rule is recommended:

"A ball lying on a closely mown area *through the green* [or specify a more restricted area, e.g., at the 6th hole] may be lifted without penalty and cleaned. Before lifting the ball, the player must mark its position. Having lifted the ball, he must place it on a spot within [specify area, e.g., six inches, one club-length, etc.] of and not nearer the *hole* than where it originally lay, that is not in a *hazard* and not on a *putting green*.

A player may place his ball only once, and it is *in play* when it has been placed (Rule 20-4). If the ball fails to come to rest on the spot on which it was placed, Rule 20-3d applies. If the ball when placed comes to rest on the spot on which it is placed and it subsequently *moves*, there is no penalty and the ball must be played as it lies, unless the provisions of any other *Rule* apply.

If the player fails to mark the position of the ball before lifting it or *moves* the ball in any other manner, such as rolling it with a club, he incurs a penalty of one stroke.

Note: "Closely mown area" means any area of the *course*, including paths through the rough, cut to fairway height or less.

*PENALTY FOR BREACH OF LOCAL RULE:
<u>Match play</u> — Loss of hole; <u>Stroke play</u> — Two strokes.

*If a player incurs the general penalty for a breach of this Local Rule, no additional penalty under the Local Rule is applied."

d. Aeration Holes

When a *course* has been aerated, a Local Rule permitting relief, without penalty, from an aeration hole may be warranted. The following Local Rule is recommended:

"*Through the green*, a ball that comes to rest in or on an aeration hole may be lifted without penalty, cleaned and dropped as near as possible to the spot where it lay but not nearer the *hole*. The ball when dropped must first strike a part of the *course through the green*.

On the *putting green*, a ball that comes to rest in or on an aeration hole may be placed at the nearest spot not nearer the *hole* that avoids the situation.

PENALTY FOR BREACH OF LOCAL RULE:
<u>Match play</u> — Loss of hole; <u>Stroke play</u> — Two strokes."

e. Seams of Cut Turf

If a *Committee* wishes to allow relief from seams of cut turf, but not from the cut turf itself, the following Local Rule is recommended:

"*Through the green*, seams of cut turf (not the turf itself) are deemed to be *ground under repair*. However, interference by a seam with the player's *stance* is deemed not to be, of itself, interference under Rule 25-1. If the ball lies in or touches the seam or the seam interferes with the area of intended swing, relief is available under Rule 25-1. All seams within the cut turf area are considered the same seam.

PENALTY FOR BREACH OF LOCAL RULE:
<u>Match play</u> — Loss of hole; <u>Stroke play</u> — Two strokes."

5. Stones in Bunkers

Stones are, by definition, *loose impediments* and, when a player's ball is in a *hazard*, a stone lying in or touching the *hazard* may not be touched or moved (Rule 13-4). However, stones in *bunkers* may represent a danger to players (a player could be injured by a stone struck by the player's club in an attempt to play the ball) and they may interfere with the proper playing of the game.

When permission to lift a stone in a *bunker* is warranted, the following Local Rule is recommended:

"Stones in *bunkers* are movable *obstructions* (Rule 24-1 applies)."

6. Immovable Obstructions Close to Putting Green

Rule 24-2 provides relief, without penalty, from interference by an immovable *obstruction,* but also provides that, except on the *putting green,* intervention on the *line of play* is not, of itself, interference under this Rule.

However, on some courses, the aprons of the *putting greens* are so closely mown that players may wish to putt from just off the green. In such conditions, immovable *obstructions* on the apron may interfere with the proper playing of the game and the introduction of the following Local Rule providing additional relief, without penalty, from intervention by an immovable *obstruction* would be warranted:

"Relief from interference by an immovable *obstruction* may be taken under Rule 24-2. In addition, if a ball lies off the *putting green* but not in a *hazard* and an immovable *obstruction* on or within two club-lengths of the *putting green* and within two club-lengths of the ball intervenes on the *line of play* between the ball and the *hole,* the player may take relief as follows:

The ball must be lifted and dropped at the nearest point to where the ball lay that (a) is not nearer the *hole,* (b) avoids intervention and (c) is not in a *hazard* or on a *putting green.*

The ball may be cleaned when lifted.

Relief under this Local Rule is also available if the player's ball lies on the *putting green* and an immovable *obstruction* within two club-lengths of the *putting green* intervenes on his *line of putt.* The player may take relief as follows:

The ball must be lifted and placed at the nearest point to where the ball lay that (a) is not nearer the *hole,* (b) avoids intervention and (c) is not in a *hazard.* The ball may be cleaned when lifted.

PENALTY FOR BREACH OF LOCAL RULE:
Match play — Loss of hole; Stroke play — Two strokes."

7. Temporary Obstructions

When temporary obstructions are installed on or adjoining the *course,* the *Committee* should define the status of such obstructions as movable, immovable or temporary immovable obstructions.

a. Temporary Immovable Obstructions

If the *Committee* defines such obstructions as temporary immovable obstructions, the following Local Rule is recommended:

"I. Definition
A temporary immovable obstruction (TIO) is a non-permanent artificial object that is often erected in conjunction with a competition and is fixed or not readily movable.

Examples of TIOs include, but are not limited to, tents, scoreboards, grandstands, television towers and lavatories.

Supporting guy wires are part of the TIO, unless the *Committee* declares that they are to be treated as elevated power lines or cables.

II. Interference
Interference by a TIO occurs when (a) the ball lies in front of and so close to the TIO that the TIO interferes with the player's *stance* or the area of his intended swing, or (b) the ball lies in, on, under or behind the TIO so that any part of the TIO intervenes directly between the player's ball and

the *hole* and is on his *line of play*; interference also exists if the ball lies within one club-length of a spot equidistant from the *hole* where such intervention would exist.

Note: A ball is under a TIO when it is below the outermost edges of the TIO, even if these edges do not extend downwards to the ground.

III. Relief

A player may obtain relief from interference by a TIO, including a TIO that is *out of bounds*, as follows:

(a) Through the Green: If the ball lies *through the green*, the point on the *course* nearest to where the ball lies must be determined that (a) is not nearer the *hole*, (b) avoids interference as defined in Clause II and (c) is not in a *hazard* or on a *putting green*. The player must lift the ball and drop it, without penalty, within one club-length of the point so determined on a part of the *course* that fulfills (a), (b) and (c) above.

(b) In a Hazard: If the ball is in a *hazard*, the player must lift and drop the ball either:

(i) Without penalty, in accordance with Clause III(a) above, except that the nearest part of the *course* affording complete relief must be in the *hazard* and the ball must be dropped in the *hazard*, or, if complete relief is impossible, on a part of the *course* within the *hazard* that affords maximum available relief; or

(ii) Under penalty of one stroke, outside the *hazard* as follows: the point on the *course* nearest to where the ball lies must be determined that (a) is not nearer the *hole*, (b) avoids interference as defined in Clause II and (c) is not in a *hazard*. The player must drop the ball within one club-length of the point so determined on a part of the *course* that fulfills (a), (b) and (c) above.

The ball may be cleaned when lifted under Clause III.

Note 1: If the ball lies in a *hazard*, nothing in this Local Rule precludes the player from proceeding under Rule 26 or Rule 28, if applicable.

Note 2: If a ball to be dropped under this Local Rule is not immediately recoverable, another ball may be *substituted*.

Note 3: A *Committee* may make a Local Rule (a) permitting or requiring a player to use a Dropping Zone when taking relief from a TIO or (b) permitting a player, as an additional relief option, to drop the ball on the opposite side of the TIO from the point established under Clause III, but otherwise in accordance with Clause III.

Exceptions:
If a player's ball lies in front of or behind the TIO (not in, on or under the *obstruction*), he may not obtain relief under Clause III if:

1. It is clearly unreasonable for him to make a *stroke* or, in the case of intervention, to make a *stroke* such that the ball could finish on a direct line to the *hole*, because of interference by anything other than the TIO;

2. Interference by the TIO would occur only through use of an unnecessarily abnormal *stance*, swing or direction of play; or

3. In the case of intervention, it would be clearly unreasonable to expect the player to be able to strike the ball far enough toward the *hole* to reach the TIO.

A player not entitled to relief due to these exceptions may proceed under Rule 24-2, if applicable.

IV. Ball in TIO Not Found

If it is known or virtually certain that a ball that has not been found is in, on or under a TIO, a ball may be dropped under the provisions of Clause III or Clause V, if applicable.

For the purpose of applying Clauses III and V, the ball is deemed to lie at the spot where it last crossed the outermost limits of the TIO (Rule 24-3).

V. Dropping Zones

If the player has interference from a TIO, the *Committee* may permit or require the use of a Dropping Zone. If the player uses a Dropping Zone in taking relief, he must drop the ball in the Dropping Zone nearest to where his ball originally lay or is deemed to lie under Clause IV (even though the nearest Dropping Zone may be nearer the *hole*).

Note: A *Committee* may make a Local Rule prohibiting the use of a Dropping Zone that is nearer the *hole*.

PENALTY FOR BREACH OF LOCAL RULE:
<u>Match play</u> — Loss of hole; <u>Stroke play</u> — Two strokes."

b. Temporary Power Lines and Cables

When temporary power lines, cables or telephone lines are installed on the *course*, the following Local Rule is recommended:

"Temporary power lines, cables, telephone lines and mats covering or stanchions supporting them are *obstructions*:

1. If they are readily movable, Rule 24-1 applies.

2. If they are fixed or not readily movable, the player may, if the ball lies *through the green* or in a *bunker*, obtain relief as provided in Rule 24-2b. If the ball lies in a *water hazard*, the player may lift and drop the ball in accordance with Rule 24-2b(i), except that the *nearest point of relief* must be in the *water hazard* and the ball must be dropped in the *water hazard* or the player may proceed under Rule 26.

3. If a ball strikes an elevated power line or cable, the *stroke* must be canceled and replayed, without penalty (see Rule 20-5). If the ball is not immediately recoverable, another ball may be *substituted*.

    Note: Guy wires supporting a temporary immovable obstruction are part of the temporary immovable obstruction, unless the *Committee*, by Local Rule, declares that they are to be treated as elevated power lines or cables.

Exception: A *stroke* that results in a ball striking an elevated junction section of cable rising from the ground must not be replayed.

4. Grass-covered cable trenches are *ground under repair,* even if not marked, and Rule 25-1b applies."

8. Dropping Zones

If the *Committee* considers that it is not feasible or practicable to proceed in accordance with a Rule providing relief, it may establish Dropping Zones in which balls may or must be dropped when taking relief. Generally, such Dropping Zones should be provided as an additional relief option to those available under the Rule itself, rather than being mandatory.

Using the example of a Dropping Zone for a *water hazard,* when such a Dropping Zone is established, the following Local Rule is recommended:

"If a ball is in or it is known or virtually certain that a ball that has not been found is in the *water hazard* (specify location), the player may:

(i) proceed under Rule 26; or

(ii) as an additional option, drop a ball, under penalty of one stroke, in the Dropping Zone.

PENALTY FOR BREACH OF LOCAL RULE:
Match play — Loss of hole; Stroke play — Two strokes."

Note: When using a Dropping Zone the following provisions apply regarding the dropping and re-dropping of the ball:

(a) The player does not have to stand within the Dropping Zone when dropping the ball.

(b) The dropped ball must first strike a part of the *course* within the Dropping Zone.

(c) If the Dropping Zone is defined by a line, the line is within the Dropping Zone.

(d) The dropped ball does not have to come to rest within the Dropping Zone.

(e) The dropped ball must be re-dropped if it rolls and comes to rest in a position covered by Rule 20-2c(i-vi).

(f) The dropped ball may roll nearer the hole than the spot where it first struck a part of the *course*, provided it comes to rest within two club-lengths of that spot and not into any of the positions covered by (e).

(g) Subject to the provisions of (e) and (f), the dropped ball may roll and come to rest nearer the hole than:

- its original position or estimated position (see Rule 20-2b);
- the *nearest point of relief* or maximum available relief (Rule 24-2, 24-3, 25-1 or 25-3); or
- the point where the original ball last crossed the margin of the *water hazard* or *lateral water hazard* (Rule 26-1).

9. Distance-Measuring Devices

If the *Committee* wishes to act in accordance with the Note under Rule 14-3, the following wording is recommended:

"Distance-Measuring Devices:

[Specify as appropriate, e.g., In this competition, or For all play at this *course*, etc.], a player may obtain distance information by using a device that measures distance only. If, during a *stipulated round*, a player uses a distance-measuring device that is designed to gauge or measure other conditions that might affect his play (e.g., gradient, wind speed, temperature, etc.), the player is in breach of Rule 14-3, for which the penalty is disqualification, regardless of whether any such additional function is actually used."

PART C:
CONDITIONS OF THE COMPETITION

Rule 33-1 provides, "The *Committee* must establish the conditions under which a competition is to be played." These conditions should include many matters such as method of entry, eligibility, number of rounds to be played, etc., which it is not appropriate to deal with in the Rules of Golf or this Appendix. Detailed information regarding these conditions is provided in "Decisions on the Rules of Golf" under Rule 33-1 and in "How to Conduct a Competition."

However, there are a number of matters that might be covered in the Conditions of the Competition to which the *Committee*'s attention is specifically drawn. These are:

1. Specifications of Clubs and the Ball

The following conditions are recommended only for competitions involving expert players:

a. List of Conforming Driver Heads

On its Web site (http://www.usga.org) the USGA periodically issues a List of Conforming Driver Heads that lists driving clubheads that have been evaluated and found to conform to the Rules of Golf. If the *Committee* wishes to limit players to drivers that have a clubhead, identified by model and loft, that is on the List, the List should be made available and the following condition of competition used:

"Any driver the player carries must have a clubhead, identified by model and loft, that is named on the current List of Conforming Driver Heads issued by the USGA.

Exception: A driver with a clubhead that was manufactured prior to 1999 is exempt from this condition.

*PENALTY FOR CARRYING, BUT NOT MAKING STROKE WITH, CLUB OR CLUBS IN BREACH OF CONDITION:
Match play — At the conclusion of the hole at which the breach is discovered, the state of the match is adjusted by

deducting one hole for each hole at which a breach occurred; maximum deduction per round — Two holes.

<u>Stroke play</u> — Two strokes for each hole at which any breach occurred; maximum penalty per round — Four strokes.

<u>Match or stroke play</u> — In the event of a breach between the play of two holes, the penalty applies to the next hole.

<u>Bogey and par competitions</u> — See Note 1 to Rule 32-1a.

<u>Stableford competitions</u> — See Note 1 to Rule 32-1b.

*Any club or clubs carried in breach of this condition must be declared out of play by the player to his opponent in match play or his *marker* or a *fellow-competitor* in stroke play immediately upon discovery that a breach has occurred. If the player fails to do so, he is disqualified.

PENALTY FOR MAKING STROKE WITH CLUB IN BREACH OF CONDITION:
Disqualification."

b. List of Conforming Golf Balls

On its Web site (http://www.usga.org) the USGA periodically issues a List of Conforming Golf Balls that lists balls that have been tested and found to conform with the Rules of Golf. If the *Committee* wishes to require players to play a brand and model of golf ball on the List, the List should be made available and the following condition of competition used:

"The ball the player plays must be named on the current List of Conforming Golf Balls issued by the United States Golf Association.

PENALTY FOR BREACH OF CONDITION:
Disqualification."

c. One Ball Condition

If it is desired to prohibit changing brands and models of golf balls during a *stipulated round*, the following condition is recommended:

"Limitation on Balls Used During Round (Note to Rule 5-1):

(i) One Ball Condition

During a *stipulated round*, the balls a player plays must

be of the same brand and model as detailed by a single entry on the current List of Conforming Golf Balls.

Note: If a ball of a different brand and/or model is dropped or placed, it may be lifted, without penalty, and the player must then proceed by dropping or placing a proper ball (Rule 20-6).

PENALTY FOR BREACH OF CONDITION:

Match play — At the conclusion of the hole at which the breach is discovered, the state of the match is adjusted by deducting one hole for each hole at which a breach occurred; maximum deduction per round — Two holes.

Stroke play — Two strokes for each hole at which any breach occurred; maximum penalty per round — Four strokes.

(ii) Procedure When Breach Discovered

When a player discovers that he has played a ball in breach of this condition, he must abandon that ball before playing from the next *teeing ground* and complete the round with a proper ball; otherwise, the player is disqualified. If discovery is made during play of a hole and the player elects to *substitute* a proper ball before completing that hole, the player must place a proper ball on the spot where the ball played in breach of the condition lay."

2. Time of Starting (Note to Rule 6-3a)

If the *Committee* wishes to act in accordance with the Note, the following wording is recommended:

"If the player arrives at his starting point, ready to play, within five minutes after his starting time, in the absence of circumstances that warrant waiving the penalty of disqualification as provided in Rule 33-7, the penalty for failure to start on time is loss of the first hole to be played in match play or two strokes in stroke play. Penalty for lateness beyond five minutes is disqualification."

3. Caddie (Note to Rule 6-4)

Rule 6-4 permits a player to use a *caddie*, provided he has only one *caddie* at any one time. However, there may be circumstances where a *Committee* may wish to prohibit *caddies* or restrict a player in his choice of *caddie,* e.g., professional golfer, sibling, parent, another player in the competition, etc. In such cases, the following wording is recommended:

Use of Caddie Prohibited
"A player is prohibited from using a *caddie* during the *stipulated round.*"

Restriction on Who May Serve as Caddie
"A player is prohibited from having _____ serve as his *caddie* during the *stipulated round.*

PENALTY FOR BREACH OF CONDITION:

<u>Match play</u> — At the conclusion of the hole at which the breach is discovered, the state of the match is adjusted by deducting one hole for each hole at which a breach occurred; maximum deduction per round — Two holes.

<u>Stroke play</u> — Two strokes for each hole at which any breach occurred; maximum penalty per round — Four strokes.

<u>Match or stroke play</u> — In the event of a breach between the play of two holes, the penalty applies to the next hole.

A player having a *caddie* in breach of this condition must immediately upon discovery that a breach has occurred ensure that he conforms with this condition for the remainder of the *stipulated round.* Otherwise, the player is disqualified."

4. Pace of Play (Note 2 to Rule 6-7)

The *Committee* may establish pace of play guidelines to help prevent slow play, in accordance with Note 2 to Rule 6-7.

5. Suspension of Play Due to a Dangerous Situation (Note to Rule 6-8b)

As there have been many deaths and injuries from lightning on golf courses, all clubs and sponsors of golf competitions are urged to take precautions for the protection of persons against lightning. Attention is called to Rules 6-8 and 33-2d. If the *Committee* desires to adopt the condition in the Note under Rule 6-8b, the following wording is recommended:

"When play is suspended by the *Committee* for a dangerous

situation, if the players in a match or group are between the play of two holes, they must not resume play until the *Committee* has ordered a resumption of play. If they are in the process of playing a hole, they must discontinue play immediately and not resume play until the *Committee* has ordered a resumption of play. If a player fails to discontinue play immediately, he is disqualified, unless circumstances warrant waiving the penalty as provided in Rule 33-7.

The signal for suspending play due to a dangerous situation will be a prolonged note of the siren."

The following signals are generally used and it is recommended that all *Committees* do similarly:

- **Discontinue Play Immediately:**
  One prolonged note of siren.
- **Discontinue Play:**
  Three consecutive notes of siren, repeated.
- **Resume Play:** Two short notes of siren, repeated.

6. Practice

a. General

The *Committee* may make regulations governing practice in accordance with the Note to Rule 7-1, Exception (c) to Rule 7-2, Note 2 to Rule 7 and Rule 33-2c.

b. Practice Between Holes (Note 2 to Rule 7)

If the *Committee* wishes to act in accordance with Note 2 to Rule 7-2, the following wording is recommended:

"Between the play of two holes, a player must not make any practice *stroke* on or near the *putting green* of the hole last played and must not test the surface of the *putting green* of the hole last played by rolling a ball.

PENALTY FOR BREACH OF CONDITION:

Match play — Loss of next hole.
Stroke play — Two strokes at the next hole.
Match or stroke play — In the case of a breach at the last hole of the *stipulated round*, the player incurs the penalty at that hole."

7. Advice in Team Competitions (Note to Rule 8)

If the *Committee* wishes to act in accordance with the Note under Rule 8, the following wording is recommended:

"In accordance with the Note to Rule 8 of the Rules of Golf, each team may appoint one person (in addition to the persons from whom *advice* may be asked under that *Rule*) who may give *advice* to members of that team. Such person (if it is desired to insert any restriction on who may be nominated, insert such restriction here) must be identified to the *Committee* before giving *advice*."

8. New Holes (Note to Rule 33-2b)

The *Committee* may provide, in accordance with the Note to Rule 33-2b, that the *holes* and *teeing grounds* for a single-round competition being held on more than one day may be differently situated on each day.

9. Transportation

If it is desired to require players to walk in a competition, the following condition is recommended:

"Players must not ride on any form of transportation during a *stipulated round* unless authorized by the *Committee*.

PENALTY FOR BREACH OF CONDITION:

Match play — At the conclusion of the hole at which the breach is discovered, the state of the match is adjusted by deducting one hole for each hole at which a breach occurred; maximum deduction per round: Two holes.

Stroke play — Two strokes for each hole at which any breach occurred; maximum penalty per round: Four strokes.

Match or stroke play — In the event of a breach between the play of two holes, the penalty applies to the next hole. Use of any unauthorized form of transportation must be discontinued immediately upon discovery that a breach has occurred. Otherwise, the player is disqualified."

10. Anti-Doping

The *Committee* may require, in the conditions of competition, that players comply with an anti-doping policy.

11. How to Decide Ties

In both match play and stroke play, a tie can be an acceptable result. However, when it is desired to have a sole winner, the *Committee* has the authority, under Rule 33-6, to determine how and when a tie is decided. The decision should be published in advance.

The USGA recommends:

Match Play

A match that ends all square should be played off hole by hole until one *side* wins a hole. The play-off should start on the hole where the match began. In a handicap match, handicap strokes should be allowed as in the *stipulated round*.

Stroke Play

(a) In the event of a tie in a scratch stroke-play competition, a play-off is recommended. The play-off may be over 18 holes or a smaller number of holes as specified by the *Committee*. If that is not feasible or there is still a tie, a hole-by-hole play-off is recommended.

(b) In the event of a tie in a handicap stroke-play competition, a play-off with handicaps is recommended. The play-off may be over 18 holes or a smaller number of holes as specified by the *Committee*. It is recommended that any such play-off consist of at least three holes.

In competitions where the handicap stroke allocation table is not relevant, if the play-off is less than 18 holes the percentage of 18 holes played should be applied to the players' handicaps to determine their play-off handicaps. Handicap stroke fractions of one-half stroke or more should count as a full stroke and any lesser fraction should be disregarded.

In competitions where the handicap stroke table is relevant, such as four-ball stroke play and bogey, par and

Stableford competitions, handicap strokes should be taken as they were assigned for the competition using the players' respective stroke allocation table(s).

(c) If a play-off of any type is not feasible, matching score cards is recommended. The method of matching cards should be announced in advance and should also provide what will happen if this procedure does not produce a winner. An acceptable method of matching the cards is to determine the winner on the basis of the best score for the last nine holes. If the tying players have the same score for the last nine, determine the winner on the basis of the last six holes, last three holes and finally the 18th hole. If this method is used in a competition with a multiple tee start, it is recommended that the "last nine holes, last six holes, etc." is considered to be holes 10-18, 13-18, etc.

For competitions where the handicap stroke table is not relevant, such as individual stroke play, if the last nine, last six, last three holes scenario is used, one-half, one-third, one-sixth, etc. of the handicaps should be deducted from the score for those holes. In terms of the use of fractions in such deductions, the *Committee* should act in accordance with the recommendations of the relevant handicapping authority.

In competitions where the handicap stroke table is relevant, such as *four-ball* stroke play and bogey, par and Stableford competitions, handicap strokes should be taken as they were assigned for the competition, using the players' respective stroke allocation table(s).

12. Draw for Match Play

Although the draw for match play may be completely blind or certain players may be distributed through different quarters or eighths, the General Numerical Draw is recommended if matches are determined by a qualifying round.

General Numerical Draw

For purposes of determining places in the draw, ties in qualifying rounds other than those for the last qualifying place are decided by the order in which scores are returned, with the first score to be returned receiving the lowest available number, etc. If it is impossible to determine the order in which scores are returned, ties are determined by a blind draw.

UPPER HALF	LOWER HALF	UPPER HALF	LOWER HALF
64 QUALIFIERS		**32 QUALIFIERS**	
1 vs. 64	2 vs. 63	1 vs. 32	2 vs. 31
32 vs. 33	31 vs. 34	16 vs. 17	15 vs. 18
16 vs. 49	15 vs. 50	8 vs. 25	7 vs. 26
17 vs. 48	18 vs. 47	9 vs. 24	10 vs. 23
8 vs. 57	7 vs. 58	4 vs. 29	3 vs. 30
25 vs. 40	26 vs. 39	13 vs. 20	14 vs. 19
9 vs. 56	10 vs. 55	5 vs. 28	6 vs. 27
24 vs. 41	23 vs. 42	12 vs. 21	11 vs. 22
4 vs. 61	3 vs. 62	**16 QUALIFIERS**	
29 vs. 36	30 vs. 35	1 vs. 16	2 vs. 15
13 vs. 52	14 vs. 51	8 vs. 9	7 vs. 10
20 vs. 45	19 vs. 46	4 vs. 13	3 vs. 14
5 vs. 60	6 vs. 59	5 vs. 12	6 vs. 11
28 vs. 37	27 vs. 38	**8 QUALIFIERS**	
12 vs. 53	11 vs. 54	1 vs. 8	2 vs. 7
21 vs. 44	22 vs. 43	4 vs. 5	3 vs. 6

APPENDICES II AND III

The USGA reserves the right, at any time, to change the Rules relating to clubs and balls and make or change the interpretations relating to these Rules. For up-to-date information, please contact the USGA or refer to *www.usga.org.*

Any design in a club or ball which is not covered by the Rules, which is contrary to the purpose and intent of the Rules or which might significantly change the nature of the game, will be ruled on by the USGA.

The dimensions and limits contained in Appendices II and III are given in the units by which conformance is determined. An equivalent imperial/metric conversion is also referenced for information, calculated using a conversion rate of 1 inch = 25.4 mm.

APPENDIX II DESIGN OF CLUBS

A player in doubt as to the conformity of a club should consult the USGA.

A manufacturer should submit to the USGA a sample of a club to be manufactured for a ruling as to whether the club conforms with the *Rules*. The sample becomes the property of the USGA for reference purposes. If a manufacturer fails to submit a sample or, having submitted a sample, fails to await a ruling before manufacturing and/or marketing the club, the manufacturer assumes the risk of a ruling that the club does not conform with the *Rules*.

The following paragraphs prescribe general regulations for the design of clubs, together with specifications and interpretations. Further information relating to these regulations and their proper interpretation is provided in "A Guide to the Rules on Clubs and Balls."

Where a club, or part of a club, is required to meet a specification within the *Rules,* it must be designed and manufactured with the intention of meeting that specification.

1. Clubs

a. General

A club is an implement designed to be used for striking the ball and generally comes in three forms: woods, irons and putters distinguished by shape and intended use. A putter is a club with a loft not exceeding ten degrees designed primarily for use on the putting green.

The club must not be substantially different from the traditional and customary form and make. The club must be composed of a shaft and a head and it may also have material added to the shaft to enable the player to obtain a firm hold (see 3 below). All parts of the club must be fixed so that the club is one unit, and it must have no external attachments. Exceptions may be made for attachments that do not affect the performance of the club.

b. Adjustability

All clubs may incorporate mechanisms for weight adjustment. Other forms of adjustability may also be permitted upon evaluation by the USGA. The following requirements apply to all permissible methods of adjustment:

   (i) the adjustment cannot be readily made;

   (ii) all adjustable parts are firmly fixed and there is no reasonable likelihood of them working loose during a round; and

   (iii) all configurations of adjustment conform with the Rules.

During a stipulated round, the playing characteristics of a club must not be purposely changed by adjustment or by any other means (see Rule 4-2a).

c. Length

The overall length of the club must be at least 18 inches (0.457 m) and, except for putters, must not exceed 48 inches

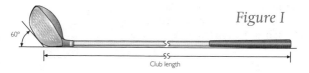

Figure I

60°

Club length

(1.219 m). For woods and irons, the measurement of length is taken when the club is lying on a horizontal plane and the sole is set against a 60 degree plane as shown in Fig. I. The length is defined as the distance from the point of the inter-section between the two planes to the top of the grip. For put-ters, the measurement of length is taken from the top of the grip along the axis of the shaft or a straight line extension of it to the sole of the club.

d. Alignment

When the club is in its normal address position the shaft must be so aligned that:

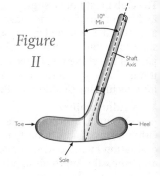

Figure II

(i) the projection of the straight part of the shaft on to the vertical plane through the toe and heel must diverge from the vertical by at least 10 degrees (see Fig. II). If the overall design of the club is such that the player can effectively use the club in a vertical or close-to-vertical position, the shaft may be required to diverge from the vertical in this plane by as much as 25 degrees;

(ii) the projection of the straight part of the shaft on to the verti-cal plane along the intended line of play must not diverge from the vertical by more than 20 degrees forward or 10 degrees backward (see Fig. III).

Figure III

Except for putters, all of the heel portion of the club must lie within 0.625 inches (15.88 mm) of the plane

containing the axis of the
straight part of the shaft
and the intended (horizontal) *line of play* (see Fig. IV).

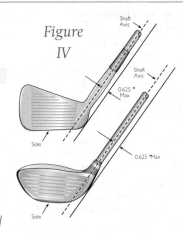

Figure IV

2. Shaft

a. Straightness

The shaft must be straight
from the top of the grip
to a point not more than
5 inches (127 mm) above
the sole, measured from
the point where the shaft
ceases to be straight along
the axis of the bent part of
the shaft and the neck and/
or socket (see Fig. V).

b. Bending and Twisting Properties

At any point along its length, the shaft must:

(i) bend in such a way that the deflection
is the same regardless of how
the shaft is rotated about its
longitudinal axis; and

(ii) twist the same amount in
both directions.

Figure V

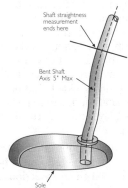

c. Attachment to Clubhead

The shaft must be attached to the clubhead at the heel either directly or through a single plain neck and/or socket. The length from the top of the neck and/or socket to the sole of the club must not exceed 5 inches (127 mm), measured along the axis of, and following any bend in, the neck and/or socket (see Fig. VI).

Figure VI

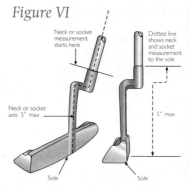

Neck or socket measurement starts here

Dotted line shows neck and socket measurement to the sole

Neck or socket axis 5" max

5" max

Sole

Sole

Exception for Putters: The shaft or neck or socket of a putter may be fixed at any point in the head.

3. Grip (see Fig. VII)

The grip consists of material added to the shaft to enable the player to obtain a firm hold. The grip must be fixed to the shaft, must be straight and plain in form, must extend to the end of the shaft and must not be molded for any part of the hands. If no material is added, that portion of the shaft designed to be held by the player must be considered the grip.

Figure VII

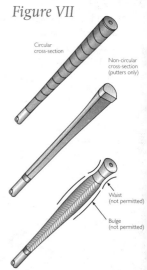

Circular cross-section

Non-circular cross-section (putters only)

Waist (not permitted)

Bulge (not permitted)

(i) For clubs other than putters the grip must be circular in cross-section, except that a continuous, straight, slightly raised rib may be incorporated along the full length of the grip, and a slightly indented spiral is permitted on a wrapped grip or a replica of one.

(ii) A putter grip may have a non-circular cross-section, provided the cross-section has no concavity, is symmetrical and remains generally similar throughout the length of the grip. (See Clause (v), below.)

(iii) The grip may be tapered but must not have any bulge or waist. Its cross-sectional dimensions measured in any direction must not exceed 1.75 inches (44.45 mm).

(iv) For clubs other than putters the axis of the grip must coincide with the axis of the shaft.

(v) A putter may have two grips, provided each is circular in cross-section, the axis of each coincides with the axis of the shaft, and they are separated by at least 1.5 inches (38 mm).

4. Clubhead

a. Plain in Shape

The clubhead must be generally plain in shape. All parts must be rigid, structural in nature and functional. The clubhead or its parts must not be designed to resemble any other object. It is not practicable to define plain in shape precisely and comprehensively. However, features which are deemed to be in breach of this requirement and are therefore not permitted include, but are not limited to:

(i) All Clubs

- holes through the face;
- holes through the head (some exceptions may be made for putters and cavity back irons);
- facsimiles of golf balls or actual golf balls incorporated into the head;
- features that are for the purpose of meeting dimensional specifications;
- features that extend into or ahead of the face;

- features that extend significantly above the top line of the head;
- furrows in or runners on the head that extend into the face (some exceptions may be made for putters); and
- optical or electronic devices.

(ii) Woods and Irons

- all features listed in (i) above;
- cavities in the outline of the heel and/or the toe of the head that can be viewed from above;
- severe or multiple cavities in the outline of the back of the head that can be viewed from above;
- transparent material added to the head with the intention of rendering conforming a feature that is not otherwise permitted; and
- features that extend beyond the outline of the head when viewed from above.

b. Dimensions, Volume and Moment of Inertia
(i) Woods

When the club is in a 60 degree lie angle, the dimensions of the clubhead must be such that:

- the distance from the heel to the toe of the clubhead is greater than the distance from the face to the back;
- the distance from the heel to the toe of the clubhead is not greater than 5 inches (127 mm); and
- the distance from the sole to the crown of the clubhead, including any permitted features, is not greater than 2.8 inches (71.12 mm).

These dimensions are measured on horizontal lines between vertical projections of the outermost points of:

- the heel and the toe; and
- the face and the back (see Fig. VIII, dimension A); and on vertical lines between the horizontal projections of

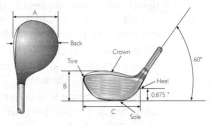

Figure VIII

the outermost points of the sole and the crown (see Fig. VIII, dimension B). If the outermost point of the heel is not clearly defined, it is deemed to be 0.875 inches (22.23 mm) above the horizontal plane on which the club is lying (see Fig. VIII, dimension C).

The volume of the clubhead must not exceed 460 cubic centimeters (28.06 cubic inches), plus a tolerance of 10 cubic centimeters (0.61 cubic inches).

When the club is in a 60 degree lie angle, the moment of inertia component around the vertical axis through the clubhead's center of gravity must not exceed 5900 g cm^2 (32.259 oz in^2), plus a test tolerance of 100 g cm^2 (0.547 oz in^2).

(ii) Irons

When the clubhead is in its normal address position, the dimensions of the head must be such that the distance from the heel to the toe is greater than the distance from the face to the back.

(iii) Putters (see Fig. IX)

When the clubhead is in its normal address position, the dimensions of the head must be such that:

- the distance from the heel to the toe is greater than the distance from the face to the back;
- the distance from the heel to the toe of the head is less than or equal to 7 inches (177.8 mm);

- the distance from the heel to the toe of the face is greater than or equal to two thirds of the distance from the face to the back of the head;

- the distance from the heel to the toe of the face is greater than or equal to half of the distance from the heel to the toe of the head;

- the distance from the sole to the top of the head, including any permitted features, is less than or equal to 2.5 inches (63.5 mm).

For traditionally shaped heads, these dimensions will be measured on horizontal lines between vertical projections of the outermost points of:

- the heel and the toe of the head;
- the heel and the toe of the face;
- the face and the back;

and on vertical lines between the horizontal projections of the outermost points of the sole and the top of the head.

For unusually shaped heads, the heel to toe measurement may be made at the face.

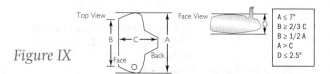

Figure IX

A ≤ 7"
B ≥ 2/3 C
B ≥ 1/2 A
A > C
D ≤ 2.5"

c. Spring Effect and Dynamic Properties

The design, material and/or construction of, or any treatment to, the clubhead (which includes the club face) must not:

(i) have the effect of a spring which exceeds the limit set forth in the Pendulum Test Protocol on file with the USGA, or

(ii) incorporate features or technology, including, but not limited to separate springs or spring features, that have the intent of, or the effect of, unduly influencing the clubhead's spring effect, or

(iii) unduly influence the movement of the ball.

Note: (i) above does not apply to putters.

d. Striking Faces

The clubhead must have only one striking face, except that a putter may have two such faces if their characteristics are the same, and they are opposite each other.

5. Club Face

a. General

The face of the club must be hard and rigid and must not impart significantly more or less spin to the ball than a standard steel face (some exceptions may be made for putters). Except for such markings listed below, the club face must be smooth and must not have any degree of concavity.

b. Impact Area Roughness and Material

Except for markings specified in the following paragraphs, the surface roughness within the area where impact is intended (the "impact area") must not exceed that of decorative sandblasting, or of fine milling (see Fig. X).

Figure X

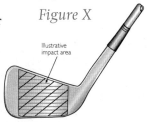

Illustrative impact area

The whole of the impact area must be of the same material (exceptions may be made for clubheads made of wood).

c. Impact Area Markings

If a club has grooves and/or punch marks in the impact area they must meet the following specifications:

(i) Grooves

- Grooves must be straight and parallel.

- Grooves must have a plain*, symmetrical cross-section and have sides which do not converge (see Fig. XI).

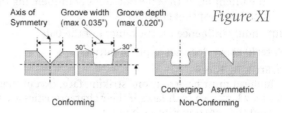

Figure XI

Conforming

Converging Asymmetric
Non-Conforming

- The width, spacing and cross-section of the grooves must be consistent throughout the impact area.
- The width (W) of each groove must not exceed 0.035 inches (0.9 mm), using the 30 degree method of measurement on file with the USGA.
- The distance between edges of adjacent grooves (S) must not be less than three times the width of the grooves, and not less than 0.075 inches (1.905 mm).
- The depth of each groove must not exceed 0.020 inches (0.508 mm).
- *For clubs other than driving clubs, the cross-sectional area (A) of a groove divided by the groove pitch (W+S) must not exceed 0.0030 square inches per inch (0.0762 mm^2/mm) (see Fig. XII).

$$\frac{A}{W + S} \le 0.0030\,in^2\,/\,in$$ *Figure XII*

- Grooves must not have sharp edges or raised lips.
- *For clubs whose loft angle is greater than or equal to 25 degrees, groove edges must be substantially in the form

of a round having an effective radius which is not less than 0.010 inches (0.254 mm) when measured as shown in Fig. XIII, and not greater than 0.020 inches (0.508 mm). Deviations in effective radius within 0.001 inches (0.0254 mm) are permissible.

Figure XIII

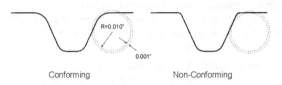

Conforming   Non-Conforming

(ii) Punch Marks

- The maximum dimension of any punch mark must not exceed 0.075 inches (1.905 mm).
- The distance between adjacent punch marks (or between punch marks and grooves) must not be less than 0.168 inches (4.27 mm), measured from center to center.
- The depth of any punch mark must not exceed 0.040 inches (1.02 mm).
- Punch marks must not have sharp edges or raised lips.
- *For clubs whose loft angle is greater than or equal to 25 degrees, punch mark edges must be substantially in the form of a round having an effective radius which is not less than 0.010 inches (0.254 mm) when measured as shown in Figure XIII, and not greater than 0.020 inches (0.508 mm). Deviations in effective radius within 0.001 inches (0.0254 mm) are permissible.

Note 1: The groove and punch mark specifications above marked with an asterisk (*) apply only to new models of clubs manufactured on or after January 1, 2010.

Note 2: Effective January 1, 2010, the Committee may require, in the conditions of competition, that the clubs the player carries must conform to the groove and punch mark specifications above marked with an asterisk (*). This condition is recommended only for competitions involving the highest level of expert player.

d. Decorative Markings

The center of the impact area may be indicated by a design within the boundary of a square whose sides are 0.375 inches (9.53 mm) in length. Such a design must not unduly influence the movement of the ball. Decorative markings are permitted outside the impact area.

e. Non-metallic Club Face Markings

The above specifications do not apply to clubheads made of wood on which the impact area of the face is of a material of hardness less than the hardness of metal and whose loft angle is 24 degrees or less, but markings which could unduly influence the movement of the ball are prohibited.

f. Putter Face Markings

Any markings on the face of a putter must not have sharp edges or raised lips. The specifications with regard to roughness, material and markings in the impact area do not apply.

APPENDIX III THE BALL

1. General

The ball must not be substantially different from the traditional and customary form and make. The material and construction of the ball must not be contrary to the purpose and intent of the Rules.

2. Weight

The weight of the ball must not be greater than 1.620 ounces avoirdupois (45.93 gm).

3. Size

The diameter of the ball must not be less than 1.680 inches (42.67 mm). This specification will be satisfied if, under its own weight, a ball falls through a 1.680 inches diameter ring gauge in fewer than 25 out of 100 randomly selected positions, the test being carried out at a temperature of $23 \pm 1°C$.

4. Spherical Symmetry

The ball must not be designed, manufactured or intentionally modified to have properties which differ from those of a spherically symmetrical ball.

5. Initial Velocity

The initial velocity of the ball must not exceed the limit specified (test on file) when measured on apparatus approved by the USGA.

6. Overall Distance Standard

The combined carry and roll of the ball, when tested on apparatus approved by the United States Golf Association, must not exceed the distance specified under the conditions set forth in the Overall Distance Standard for golf balls on file with the USGA.

RULES OF AMATEUR STATUS

Preamble

The United States Golf Association (USGA) reserves the right to change the Rules of Amateur Status and to make and change the interpretations of the Rules of Amateur Status at any time.

In the Rules of Amateur Status, the gender used in relation to any person is understood to include both genders.

DEFINITIONS

The Definitions are listed alphabetically and, in the *Rules* themselves, defined terms are in *italics*.

Amateur Golfer

An "*amateur golfer*" is one who plays the game as a non-remunerative and non-profit-making sport and who does not receive remuneration for teaching golf or for other activities because of *golf skill or reputation*, except as provided in the *Rules*.

Committee

The "*Committee*" is the Amateur Status Committee of the USGA.

Golf Skill or Reputation

It is a matter for the USGA to decide whether a particular *amateur golfer* has *golf skill or reputation*.

Generally, an *amateur golfer* is only considered to have *golf skill* if he:

(a) has had competitive success at a local or national level or has been selected to represent his national, state or regional golf association; or

(b) competes at an elite level.

Golf reputation can only be gained through *golf skill* and does not include prominence for service to the game of golf as an administrator.

Instruction

"*Instruction*" covers teaching the physical aspects of playing golf, i.e., the actual mechanics of swinging a golf club and hitting a golf ball.

Note: *Instruction* does not cover teaching the psychological aspects of the game or the Etiquette or Rules of Golf.

Junior Golfer

A *"junior golfer"* is an *amateur golfer* who has not reached (i) the September 1 following graduation from secondary school or (ii) his 19th birthday, whichever comes first.

Prize Voucher

A *"prize voucher"* is a voucher or gift certificate issued by the Committee in charge of a competition for the purchase of goods from a professional's shop or other retail source.

Retail Value

The *"retail value"* of a prize is the price at which the prize is generally available from a retail source at the time of the award.

Rule or Rules

The term *"Rule"* or *"Rules"* refers to the Rules of Amateur Status as determined by the USGA.

Symbolic Prize

A *"symbolic prize"* is a trophy made of gold, silver, ceramic, glass or the like that is permanently and distinctively engraved.

Testimonial Award

A *"testimonial award"* is an award for notable performances or contributions to golf as distinguished from competition prizes. A *testimonial award* may not be a monetary award.

Rule 1. Amateurism

1-1. General

An *amateur golfer* must play the game and conduct himself in accordance with the *Rules*.

1-2. Amateur Status

Amateur Status is a universal condition of eligibility for playing in golf competitions as an *amateur golfer*. A person who acts contrary to the *Rules* may forfeit his status as an *amateur golfer* and as a result will be ineligible to play in amateur competitions.

1-3. Purpose and Spirit of the Rules

The purpose and spirit of the *Rules* is to maintain the distinction between amateur golf and professional golf and to keep the amateur game as free as possible from the abuses that may follow from uncontrolled sponsorship and financial incentive. It is considered necessary to safeguard amateur golf, which is largely self-regulating with regard to the Rules of play and handicapping, so that it can be fully enjoyed by all *amateur golfers*.

1-4. Doubt as to Rules

A person who wishes to be an *amateur golfer* and who is in doubt as to whether taking a proposed course of action is permitted under the *Rules* should consult the USGA.

An organizer or sponsor of an amateur golf competition or a competition involving *amateur golfers* who is in doubt as to whether a proposal is in accordance with the *Rules* should consult the USGA.

Rule 2. Professionalism

2-1. General

Except as provided in the *Rules*, an *amateur golfer* must not take any action for the purpose of becoming a professional golfer and must not identify himself as a professional golfer.

Note 1: Actions by an *amateur golfer* for the purpose of becoming a professional golfer include, but are not limited to:

    (a) accepting the position of a professional golfer;

    (b) receiving services or payment, directly or indirectly, from a professional agent;

    (c) entering into a written or oral agreement, directly or indirectly, with a professional agent or sponsor; and

    (d) agreeing to accept payment or compensation, directly

or indirectly, for allowing his name or likeness as a player of *golf skill or reputation* to be used for any commercial purpose.

Note 2: An *amateur golfer* may inquire as to his likely prospects as a professional golfer, including applying unsuccessfully for the position of a professional golfer, and he may work in a professional's shop and receive payment or compensation, provided he does not infringe the *Rules* in any other way.

2-2. Membership in Professional Golfers' Organizations

a. Professional Golfers' Association

An *amateur golfer* must not hold or retain membership in any Professional Golfers' Association.

b. Professional Tours

An *amateur golfer* must not hold or retain membership in a Professional Tour limited exclusively to professional golfers.

Note: If an *amateur golfer* must compete in one or more qualifying competitions in order to be eligible for membership in a Professional Tour, he may enter and play in such qualifying competitions without forfeiting his Amateur Status, provided that, in advance of play and in writing, he waives his right to any prize money in the competition.

Rule 3. Prizes

3-1. Playing for Prize Money

An *amateur golfer* must not play golf for prize money or its equivalent in a match, competition or exhibition.

Note: An *amateur golfer* may participate in an event where prize money or its equivalent is offered, provided that prior to participation he waives his right to accept prize money in that event.

Conduct contrary to the purpose and spirit of the Rules – see Rule 7-2.)

Policy on gambling – see Appendix.)

3-2. Prize Limits

a. General

An *amateur golfer* must not accept a prize (other than a *symbolic prize*) or *prize voucher* of *retail value* in excess of $750 or the equivalent, or such a lesser figure as may be decided by the USGA. This limit applies to the total prizes or *prize vouchers* received by an *amateur golfer* in any one competition or series of competitions.

Exception: A prize, including a cash prize, for a hole-in-one made while playing golf may exceed the above prize limit.

b. Exchanging Prizes

An *amateur golfer* must not exchange a prize or *prize voucher* for cash.

Exception: An *amateur golfer* may submit a *prize voucher* to a state or regional golf association and thereafter be reimbursed from the value of that voucher for expenses incurred in participating in a golf competition, provided the reimbursement of such expenses is permitted under Rule 4-2.

Note 1: The responsibility to prove the *retail value* of a particular prize rests with the Committee in charge of the competition.

Note 2: It is recommended that the total value of prizes in a gross competition, or each division of a handicap competition, should not exceed twice the prescribed limit in an 18-hole competition, three times in a 36-hole competition, five times in a 54-hole competition and six times in a 72-hole competition.

3-3. Testimonial Awards

a. General

An *amateur golfer* must not accept a *testimonial award* of *retail value* in excess of the limits prescribed in Rule 3-2a.

b. Multiple Awards

An *amateur golfer* may accept more than one *testimonial award* from different donors, even though their total *retail value* exceeds the prescribed limit, provided they are not presented so as to evade the limit for a single award.

Rule 4. Expenses

4-1. General

Except as provided in the *Rules*, an *amateur golfer* must not accept expenses, in money or otherwise, from any source to play in a golf competition or exhibition.

4-2. Receipt of Expenses

An *amateur golfer* may receive reasonable expenses, not exceeding the actual expenses incurred, to play in a golf competition or exhibition as follows:

a. Family Support

An *amateur golfer* may receive expenses from a member of his family or a legal guardian.

b. Junior Golfers

A *junior golfer* may receive expenses when competing in a competition limited exclusively to *junior golfers*.

Note: The acceptance of expenses may violate the eligibility rules of the National Collegiate Athletic Association (NCAA).

c. Individual Events

An *amateur golfer* may receive expenses when competing in individual events, provided he complies with the following provisions:

(i) Where the competition is to take place in the United States, the expenses must be approved by and paid through the player's state or regional golf association.

(ii) Where the competition is to take place in another country, the expenses must be approved by both the USGA and the national union or association in the country in which the competition is to be staged. The expenses must be paid through the player's state or regional golf association, or, subject to the approval of the USGA, by the body controlling golf in the territory he is visiting.

The USGA may limit the receipt of expenses to a specific number of competitive days in any one calendar year, and an *amateur golfer* must not exceed any such limit. In such a case, the expenses are deemed to include reasonable travel time and practice days in connection with the competitive days.

Exception: An *amateur golfer* must not receive expenses, directly or indirectly, from a professional agent (see Rule 2-1) or any other similar source as may be determined by the USGA.

Note 1: The acceptance of expenses may violate the eligibility rules of the National Collegiate Athletic Association (NCAA).

Note 2: An *amateur golfer* of *golf skill or reputation* must not promote or advertise the source of any expenses received (see Rule 6-2).

d. Team Events

An *amateur golfer*, may receive expenses when he is representing:

- his country,
- his state or regional golf association,
- his golf club,
- his business or industry, or
- a similar body

in a team competition, practice session or training camp.

Note 1: A "similar body" includes a recognized educational institution or military service.

Note 2: Unless otherwise stated, the expenses must be paid by the body that the *amateur golfer* is representing or the body controlling golf in the country he is visiting.

e. Invitation Unrelated to Golf Skill

An *amateur golfer* who is invited for reasons unrelated to *golf skill* (e.g., a celebrity, a business associate or customer) to take part in a golf event may receive expenses.

f. Exhibitions

An *amateur golfer* who is participating in an exhibition in aid of a recognized charity may receive expenses, provided that the exhibition is not run in connection with another golfing event in which the player is competing.

g. Sponsored Handicap Competitions

An *amateur golfer* may receive expenses when competing in a sponsored handicap competition, provided the competition has been approved as follows:

(i) Where the competition is to take place in the United States, the annual approval of the USGA must first be obtained in advance by the sponsor; and

(ii) Where the competition is to take place in more than one country or involves golfers from another country, the approval of the USGA and the national union of the other country must first be obtained in advance by the sponsor. The application for this approval should be sent to the national union in the country where the competition commences when it does not commence in the United States.

Rule 5. Instruction

5-1. General

Except as provided in the *Rules*, an *amateur golfer* must not receive payment or compensation, directly or indirectly, for giving *instruction* in playing golf.

5-2. Where Payment Permitted

a. Schools, Colleges, Camps, etc.

An *amateur golfer* who is (i) an employee of an educational institution or system or (ii) a counselor at a camp or other similar organized program may receive payment or compensation for golf *instruction* to students in the institution, system or camp, provided that the total time devoted to golf *instruction* comprises less than 50 percent of the time spent in the performance of all duties as such an employee or counselor.

b. Approved Programs

An *amateur golfer* may receive expenses, payment or compensation for giving golf *instruction* as part of a program that has been approved in advance by the USGA.

5-3. Instruction in Writing

An *amateur golfer* may receive payment or compensation for golf *instruction* in writing, provided his ability or reputation as a golfer was not a major factor in his employment or in the commission or sale of his work.

Rule 6. Use of Golf Skill or Reputation

6-1. General

Except as provided in the *Rules*, an *amateur golfer* of *golf skill or reputation* must not use that skill or reputation to promote, advertise or sell anything or for any financial gain.

6-2. Lending Name or Likeness

An *amateur golfer* of *golf skill or reputation* must not use that skill or reputation to obtain payment, compensation, personal benefit or any financial gain, directly or indirectly, for allowing his name or likeness to be used for the advertisement or sale of anything.

Exception: An *amateur golfer* of *golf skill or reputation* may allow his name or likeness to be used to promote:

(a) his national, regional, state or county union or association; or

(b) (i) any golf competition or other event that is considered to be in the best interests of, or would contribute to the development of, the game or (ii) a recognized charity (or similar good cause).

The *amateur golfer* must not obtain any payment, compensation or financial gain, directly or indirectly, for doing so.

Note: An *amateur golfer* may accept golf equipment from anyone dealing in such equipment, provided no advertising is involved.

6-3. Personal Appearance

An *amateur golfer* of *golf skill or reputation* must not use that skill or reputation to obtain payment, compensation, personal benefit or any financial gain, directly or indirectly, for a personal appearance.

Exception: An *amateur golfer* may receive actual expenses in connection with a personal appearance, provided no golf competition or exhibition is involved.

6-4. Broadcasting and Writing

An *amateur golfer* of *golf skill or reputation* may receive payment, compensation, personal benefit or any financial gain from broadcasting or writing, provided:

(a) the broadcasting or writing is part of his primary occupation or career and golf *instruction* is not included (Rule 5); or

(b) the broadcasting or writing is on a part-time basis, the player is actually the author of the commentary, articles or books and *instruction* in playing golf is not included.

Note: An *amateur golfer* of *golf skill or reputation* must not promote or advertise anything within the commentary, articles or books and must not lend his name or likeness to the promotion or sale of the commentary, article or books (see Rule 6-2).

6-5. Grants and Scholarships

An *amateur golfer* of *golf skill or reputation* must not accept the benefits of a grant or scholarship, except one whose terms and conditions have been approved by the USGA.

Note: The terms and conditions of grants and scholarships provided by schools that are members of the National Collegiate Athletic Association, the Association of Intercollegiate Athletics for Women, the National Association for Intercollegiate Athletics, the National Junior College Athletic Association or other similar organizations governing athletes at academic institutions are approved by the USGA.

6-6. Membership

An *amateur golfer* of *golf skill or reputation* must not accept an offer of membership in a golf club or privileges at a golf course, without full payment for the class of membership or privilege, if such an offer is made as an inducement to play for that club or course.

Rule 7. Other Conduct Incompatible with Amateurism

7-1. Conduct Detrimental to Amateurism

An *amateur golfer* must not act in a manner that is detrimental to the best interests of the amateur game.

7-2. Conduct Contrary to the Purpose and Spirit of the Rules

An *amateur golfer* must not take any action, including actions relating to golf gambling, that is contrary to the purpose and spirit of the *Rules*.

(Policy on gambling – see Appendix.)

Rule 8. Procedure for Enforcement of the Rules

8-1. Decision on a Breach

If a possible breach of the *Rules* by a person claiming to be an *amateur golfer* comes to the attention of the *Committee*, it is a matter for the *Committee* to decide whether a breach has occurred. Each case will be investigated to the extent deemed appropriate by the *Committee* and considered on its merits. The decision of the *Committee* is final, subject to an appeal as provided in these *Rules*.

8-2. Enforcement

Upon a decision that a person has breached the *Rules*, the *Committee* may declare the Amateur Status of the person forfeited or require the person to refrain or desist from specified actions as a condition of retaining his Amateur Status.

The *Committee* should notify the person and may notify any interested golf association of any action taken under Rule 8-2.

8-3. Appeals Procedure

Any person who considers that any action he is proposing to

ake might endanger his Amateur Status may submit particu-
lars to the staff of the USGA for an advisory opinion. If dissatisfied with the staff's advisory opinion, he may, by written
notice to the staff within 30 days after being notified of the
advisory opinion, appeal to the *Committee,* in which case he
must be given reasonable notice of the *Committee's* next meeting at which the matter may be heard and must be entitled to
present his case in person or in writing. In such cases the staff
must submit to the *Committee* all information provided by the
player together with staff's findings and recommendation, and
the *Committee* must issue a decision on the matter. If dissatisfied
with the *Committee's* decision, the player may, by written notice
to the staff within 30 days after being notified of the decision,
appeal to the Executive Committee, in which case he must be
given reasonable notice of the next meeting of the Executive
Committee at which the matter may be heard and must be
entitled to present his case in person or in writing. The decision
of the Executive Committee is final.

Rule 9. Reinstatement of Amateur Status

9-1. General

The *Committee* has the sole authority to reinstate a person to
Amateur Status, prescribe a waiting period necessary for reinstatement or to deny reinstatement, subject to an appeal as provided in the *Rules.*

9-2. Applications for Reinstatement

Each application for reinstatement will be considered on its
merits, with consideration normally being given to the following principles:

a. Awaiting Reinstatement

The professional golfer is considered to hold an advantage over
the *amateur golfer* by reason of having devoted himself to the
game as his profession; other persons infringing the *Rules* also
obtain advantages not available to the *amateur golfer.* They do
not necessarily lose such advantages merely by deciding to cease

infringing the *Rules*. Therefore, an applicant for reinstatement t
Amateur Status must undergo a period awaiting reinstatement
as prescribed by the *Committee*.

The period awaiting reinstatement generally starts from the
date of the person's last breach of the *Rules* unless the *Committee*
decides that it starts from either (a) the date when the person's
last breach became known to the *Committee*, or (b) such other
date determined by the *Committee*.

b. Period Awaiting Reinstatement

(i) Professionalism

Generally, the period awaiting reinstatement is related
to the period the person was in breach of the *Rules*.
However, no applicant is normally eligible for reinstate
ment until he has conducted himself in accordance wit
the *Rules* for a period of at least one year.

It is recommended that the following guidelines on periods awaiting reinstatement be applied by the *Committee*:

Period of Breach:	Period Awaiting Reinstatement
under 5 years	1 year
5 years or more	2 years

However, the period may be extended if the applicant
has played extensively for prize money, regardless of performance. In all cases, the *Committee* reserves the right to
extend or to shorten the period awaiting reinstatement.

(ii) Other Breaches of the Rules

A period awaiting reinstatement of one year will normally be required. However, the period may be extende
if the breach is considered serious.

c. Number of Reinstatements

A person is not normally eligible to be reinstated more than
twice.

d. Players of National Prominence

A player of national prominence who has been in breach of the

Rules for more than five years is not normally eligible for reinstatement.

e. Status While Awaiting Reinstatement

An applicant for reinstatement must comply with these *Rules*, as they apply to an *amateur golfer*, during his period awaiting reinstatement.

An applicant for reinstatement is not eligible to enter competitions as an *amateur golfer*. However, he may enter competitions and win a prize solely among members of a club where he is a member, subject to the approval of the club. He must not represent such club against other clubs unless with the approval of the clubs in the competition and / or the organizing Committee.

An applicant for reinstatement may enter competitions that are not limited to *amateur golfers*, subject to the conditions of competition, without prejudicing his application, provided he does so as an applicant for reinstatement. He must waive his right to any prize money offered in the competition and must not accept any prize reserved for an *amateur golfer* (Rule 3-1).

9-3. Procedure for Applications

Each application for reinstatement must be submitted to the *Committee*, in accordance with such procedures as may be laid down and including such information as the *Committee* may require.

9-4. Appeals Procedure

See Rule 8-3.

Rule 10. Committee Decision

10-1. Committee's Decision

The *Committee's* decision is final, subject to an Appeal as provided in Rules 8-3 and 9-4.

APPENDIX — POLICY ON GAMBLING

General

An *"amateur golfer"* is one who plays the game as a non-remunerative and non-profit-making sport. Financial incentive in amateur golf, which can be the result of some forms of gambling or wagering, could give rise to abuse of the *Rules* both in play and in manipulation of handicaps that would be detrimental to the integrity of the game.

There is a distinction between playing for prize money (Rule 3-1), gambling or wagering that is contrary to the purpose and spirit of the *Rules* (Rule 7-2), and forms of gambling or wagering that do not, of themselves, breach the *Rules*. An *amateur golfer* or a Committee in charge of a competition where *amateur golfers* are competing should consult with the USGA if in any doubt as to the application of the *Rules*. In the absence of such guidance, it is recommended that no cash prizes be awarded so as to ensure that the *Rules* are upheld.

Acceptable Forms of Gambling

There is no objection to informal gambling or wagering among individual golfers or teams of golfers when it is incidental to the game. It is not practicable to define informal gambling or wagering precisely, but features that would be consistent with such gambling or wagering include:

- the players in general know each other;
- participation in the gambling or wagering is optional and is limited to the players;
- the sole source of all money won by the players is advanced by the players; and
- the amount of money involved is not generally considered to be excessive.

Therefore, informal gambling or wagering is acceptable provided the primary purpose is the playing of the game for enjoyment, not for financial gain.

Unacceptable Forms of Gambling

Other forms of gambling or wagering where there is a requirement for players to participate (e.g. compulsory sweepstakes) or that have the potential to involve considerable sums of money (e.g. calcuttas and auction sweepstakes – where players or teams are sold by auction) are not approved.

Otherwise, it is difficult to define unacceptable forms of gambling or wagering precisely, but features that would be consistent with such gambling or wagering include:

- participation in the gambling or wagering is open to non-players; and
- the amount of money involved is generally considered to be excessive.

An *amateur golfer's* participation in gambling or wagering that is not approved may be considered contrary to the purpose and spirit of the *Rules* (Rule 7-2) and may endanger his Amateur Status.

Furthermore, organized events designed or promoted to create cash prizes are not permitted. Golfers participating in such events without first irrevocably waiving their right to prize money are deemed to be playing for prize money, in breach of Rule 3-1.

Note: The Rules of Amateur Status do not apply to betting or gambling by *amateur golfers* on the results of a competition limited to or specifically organized for professional golfers.

INDEX THE RULES OF GOLF
(Items in blue relate to the Rules of Amateur Status)

THE USGA AND YOU

Contact us for:

The Rules of Golf:
For all of your Rules of Golf needs, including:

- Complete Rules of Golf and Decisions on the Rules of Golf on-line
- Frequently asked questions regarding the Rules
- Submitting your Rules questions to our experts
- Ordering Rules of Golf-related products

www.rulesofgolf.com

USGA Publication Orders:
A comprehensive selection of USGA books, pamphlets, software and videos. Publications include:

- "Decisions on the Rules of Golf — 2010-11 edition"
- Golf Rules in Brief
- Golf Rules Illustrated
- Software
- USGA Handicap Publications
- USGA Green Section Publications

www.usgapubs.com • 1-800-336-4446

USGA Shop
The ultimate source for clothing and memorabilia from our National Championships, including the U.S. Open and Women's Open, plus a full line of USGA Members clothing and accessories, golf gifts and books. USGA Member discounts available.

www.usgacatalog.com • 1-800-755-0293

USGA Members Program
Find out more about becoming a Member of the USGA and learn how your contribution will help fund a wide range of programs committed to enhance your enjoyment of the game while ensuring its future.

www.usga.org • 1-800-223-0041